ADLESTROP
REVISITED

AN ANTHOLOGY INSPIRED BY
EDWARD THOMAS'S POEM

COMPILED AND EDITED BY

ANNE HARVEY

SUTTON PUBLISHING

First published in the United Kingdom in 1999 by
Sutton Publishing Limited · Phoenix Mill
Thrupp · Stroud · Gloucestershire · GL5 2BU

British Library Cataloguing in Publication Data
A catalogue record for this book is available from the British Library

ISBN 0 7509 2289 3

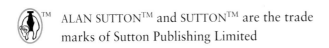

ALAN SUTTON™ and SUTTON™ are the trade marks of Sutton Publishing Limited

Typeset in 10/14 pt Sabon.
Typesetting and origination by
Sutton Publishing Limited.
Printed in Great Britain by
Redwood Books, Trowbridge, Wiltshire.

We made a number of excursions together, taking bicycles and putting up haphazard at inns – Avebury, Swindon, Malmesbury, Stroud, Westbury, Bridgwater, Selborne and other places. One of these journeys is recorded in a book he wrote, *In Pursuit of Spring*. . . .

As an illustration of his extraordinary talent for giving an intense significance to a single, almost momentary, experience, I recall on that occasion lying on the beach at Kilve. We had confirmed the fact that there was no weathercock on the church, and were resting in peace and almost in silence. Then he turned and bade me listen. A little melodious twitter sounded somewhere, and a tiny bird dipped and swooped between us and the sea. 'A meadow pipit,' he said, and the moment became unforgettable.

from *Edward – a memoir*
by Jesse Berridge

DEDICATION
*To the memory of the late Ramon Willey
who explored the poem and the place
before I did, and to Dorothy Price
'the First Lady of Adlestrop'.*

Thomas Bewick

CONTENTS

Adlestrop

Yes. I remember Adlestrop—
The name, because one afternoon
Of heat the express-train drew up there
Unwontedly. It was late June.

The steam hissed. Someone cleared his throat.
No one left and no one came
On the bare platform. What I saw
Was Adlestrop—only the name

And willows, willow-herb, and grass,
And meadowsweet, and haycocks dry,
No whit less still and lonely fair
Than the high cloudlets in the sky.

And for that minute a blackbird sang
Close by, and round him, mistier,
Farther and farther, all the birds
Of Oxfordshire and Gloucestershire.

EDWARD THOMAS

James Bostock

John Wheatley

Letter to Robert Frost from Hare Hall Camp, 16 March 1916:

> . . . It IS warm today. We have a day with no work (but plenty to consider) and 2 of us are left in the parlour of 'The Shepherd and Dog' 2 miles from camp, a public house rather like that one at Tyler's Green or Penn. I am writing this and the other man, who is an artist, is trying to draw me. He is the man through whom I fell into disgrace. I haven't outlived it yet. . . .

This last comment was explained in a letter to Gordon Bottomley from the camp on 11 February:

> . . . I was to have been made a corporal 3 weeks ago, but I had got into trouble for reporting a man present whom I expected in 'every minute'. The sergeant major wouldn't hear of my promotion after that, so it may be an age, it may be only in the next war, before I wear 3 stripes & a bayonet which were naturally my one ambition.

After leaving the Artists' Rifles, John Wheatley was later a Ministry of Information War Artist.

INTRODUCTION

In 1991 I edited *Elected Friends*, an anthology of poems written for and about the poet Edward Thomas, surprising myself and others that a writer once so neglected should have influenced so many poets. I realised then that one poem, 'Adlestrop', had been a particular inspiration.

The Edward Thomas Fellowship holds an annual seminar, and looking for a subject for 1998 'Adlestrop' came to mind. The amount of material that the research yielded has led to this book.

I have gathered all that seems curious, relevant, coincidental and intriguing, which I hope will both entertain and illuminate a poem written eighty-five years ago, and continuing its journey today.

Edward Thomas was born in 1878, one of six brothers and of Welsh ancestry. The South London countryside of his childhood provided an early love of walking and wildlife. At St Paul's School he wrote on the fly-leaf of an algebra book, 'and in the worst possible Latin, I LIKE BIRDS MORE THAN BOOKS'. He loved books too,

The Thomas family when Edward was at St Paul's School, *c.* 1894–5. From left to right: his father, Julian, Ernest, Edward, Reggie, Oscar, Dory (Theodore), and his mother.

read widely, and published his first book, *The Woodland Life*, while still at Oxford. He married his childhood sweetheart, Helen Noble, in 1899 and they had three children. Although supporting his family by writing he found the nature of the work depressing – hack-work journalism, dull biographies, reviews of books that held no interest. 'Literature, we call it in Fleet Street,' he said 'derived from Litter.'

Overwork and pressing deadlines led to a breakdown, and he suffered frequent, often severe, depression. But he underrated himself always: some of his finest prose is today being reissued to reach new readers, and he was revered as a leading critic of poetry.

There was, too, a different side to this complex man. His family and friends would remember his sense of humour; companionship; delightful, rare talk; enjoyment in games and songs. His circle of friends was wide; some feature in this book, notably the writers Gordon Bottomley, Eleanor Farjeon and Robert Frost.

Writing on Edward Thomas and 'Adlestrop' one is conscious of Time and Coincidence. W.H. Hudson had felt of Thomas that 'He has taken the wrong path and is wandering lost in the vast wilderness. He is essentially a poet'; and Eleanor Farjeon, after reading his essays 'Light and Twilight', had asked him, tentatively, 'Haven't you ever written poetry, Edward?'

'Me? I couldn't write a poem to save my life' came the reply.

The meeting with the American Robert Frost, over here to further his own career, happened at the right time. The rapport between them, their shared interest in poetry, brought the confidence Thomas needed. The friendship began in London and a vital phase in it was the holiday of August 1914, not long after the Adlestrop journey. Frost and Thomas were briefly, but importantly, part of the group whom the Gloucester solicitor John Haines named The Dymock Poets, linking place and poetry. Eighty-five years later some new roads in the Ledbury area would be named after Gibson, Abercrombie, Drinkwater, Brooke, Frost and Thomas.

All 144 of Edward Thomas's poems were written in the two years following that August. 'Adlestrop', one of those poems, has taken on a special significance: written at the start of the war that would change England irrevocably, and in which Thomas would die . . . written about a railway station that is no longer there . . . about a Cotswold village that many discover because of the poem, although the poet himself never went there.

If I needed encouragement to pursue my idea, I had to look no further than the comments in the Visitors' Book in the Church of St Mary Magdalene.

> 'I came because of the poem. . . .'
> 'Our wrong turning has turned out right.'
> 'I hadn't realised there was an Adlestrop until I read
>   the poem. . . .'
> 'I remember teaching Adlestrop. . . . I hope my pupils do!'
> 'Thank you, Edward Thomas. I <u>will</u> remember Adlestrop.'

Anne Harvey
April 1999

The Imaginative Franchise

JOHN LOVEDAY

'. . . *the peculiar truth of poetry may have to be rendered by fictions, or by*
what, literally, amounts to lies . . . '
Michael Hamburger, *The Truth of Poetry*

Does it matter, whether Yeats really stood
Among schoolchildren? Lawrence's snake
Could as easily have slithered out of his skull
As out of that fissure. Were there woods
Frost stopped his horse by, and did there fall
The 'darkest evening'? Had Larkin a bike?
Does it have to be true? Suppose the train did not pull
Up at Adlestrop at all . . .

1986

Train of Thought

ANNE HARVEY

'Adlestrop' . . . a poem equally loved by railway buffs, country lovers, children
and the literati. A simple 16-line poem evoking a moment that we, too, have
experienced somewhere, sometime . . . a moment almost forgotten . . . nostalgic in
an indefinable way. And it could simply rest there . . . except . . . my curiosity was
aroused following a conversation about the poem:

It was late June, wasn't it? 1914. . . . Does anyone know which date?
I think I read somewhere . . . the 23rd.
Oh, was it? The 23rd? . . . And the express train drew up there, didn't it?
Unwontedly . . . odd word.
Unexpectedly.
I like 'unwontedly'. . . . Were there express trains in 1914 . . . on the . . .
which line was it?

The Paddington to Worcester . . . Great Western Railway . . . Oxford, Worcester, Wolverhampton . . . nicknamed the Old Worse and Worse . . .

And there WERE express trains in 1914?

Yes . . . I think so. . . . I haven't ever seen a timetable, but . . .

So . . . was he going down to Worcester . . . or up to London? . . . And was his wife with him? Or was he alone?

Oh, alone. . . . I mean, you can tell that, can't you . . . from the poem . . . the whole mood of it . . . and he does say 'What I saw was Adlestrop . . .

Yes, but poets don't always . . .

And anyway, it was June . . . still term-time. His wife . . . Helen . . . will have been looking after the children . . . and he was on his way to Robert Frost . . . up near Ledbury. . . . Helen didn't meet the Frosts until later . . . when war began . . . August . . . she wrote about it.

And yet . . . had I read conflicting accounts of this now famous railway journey? Half-remembered anecdotes and dates were confused in my mind. 'Yes. I remember Adlestrop, the name—because . . .'

Buried among my papers was an article by Simon Hoggart in which he told *Guardian* readers:

The most famous thing in Adlestrop is its station sign, the villagers have set it up in the bus shelter . . . a plaque let into a bench has the poem printed on it. There are bus shelters remembering aldermen and those who fell in world wars, but this is probably the only one which commemorates a poem. . . .

Then came this inviting paragraph:

A visit to the station provides the opportunity for a little literary detective work; trifling enough but surely adequate to keep a PhD student busy for a year or so, fresh subjects being in such short supply. . . . For a start it should be possible to work out exactly where Thomas's compartment was when the train stopped. It seems likely that he was travelling south to London. . . .

[Except that he wasn't!]

. . . if he had been at the southern end of the platform, by the bridge which carries the road from Stow-on-the-Wold, he could have spotted a willow . . . fifty yards to the north, he would have had an uninterrupted view of the meadows and the haycocks . . . of course, if he was too far down the line, he would not have been able to read the station sign.

A real modern literary sleuth would have discovered whether Thomas travelled first-class, which end of the train the first-class compartments were, whether there were signals on the line at this point, what type of engine was pulling the train. Perhaps Thomas was travelling in the buffet car, though one suspects that the timeless moment could have been shattered by the rustle of crisp packets. . . .

Crisp packets in 1914 . . . perhaps Hoggart was joking . . . but the time was right to get down to some serious literary . . . and railway . . . detection.

I began by sorting out the various comings and goings of Helen and Edward Thomas during May and June 1914. First, May: a friend of Eleanor Farjeon offered her an old house in Kingham, Glos., during that month. Her brother, Bertie, and Joan Thornycroft, the girl he was to marry, were to stay for a week and Edward Thomas was invited to join them. He was on holiday in Wales with his two older children, Merfyn and Bronwen, when the invitation reached him, and when he replied on 25 April they were all three . . . 'In the train . . . on the way to Little Iddens . . .'

> Little Iddens
> c/o R. Frost
> Ledington,
> Ledbury,
> Hereford.

My dear Eleanor, I have been meaning to write every day since we came to Wales which we are now leaving for Herefordshire. There we expect to stay till the Friday or Saturday of next week. Then I had meant to go home on the following Tuesday. Now I should very much like to go to Kingham and think I could manage it if I spent the weekend at home putting some notebooks together etc. – if I really could work there without being a nuisance. I have worked every day since I came away and I must continue to do so, partly to keep my conscience quiet, partly because I have so much I want to get on with, especially after spending an awful lot on getting to Wales etc. Could I for instance work in the mornings and between 5 and 7.30? If so I am practically certain of coming. . . . You will like Kingham which I know a lot about, because a former sub-rector of my college lives there (and wrote a history of it later), Warde Fowler. The river positively exists . . .

A second letter, sent from the Frosts' cottage, confirms that although he will come 'It could not be before Tuesday evening, however, as I must have Tuesday in town. Can you tell me what trains there are after 4? . . .'

He arrived at Kingham on the evening of Tuesday 11 May and was given, during his stay, time for writing before breakfast and after tea. Despite descriptions of picnics, music, churchyards, games and numerous walks, there is no mention of a tiny hamlet called Adlestrop, only 3 miles away, nor of the River Evenlode, which Thomas had written about as long ago as 1902:

from

On the Evenlode

It was the season when days are so long that we must sleep lightlier than swallows, if sunset and sunrise are not to pass unsaluted. . . .

When I rose it was light, though not yet day. Alone in my room, high up among the spires, the horned turrets, the acres of dark blue gleaming slate, I took a mouthful of fruit and milk, with hopes that the summer morning would bring me somewhere pleasantly to breakfast. Then I set out. Even now the milk must be drumming yonder in the pails! The morning was already hot, so that the chill bath of shadow underneath the lindens here and there was pleasant. At the river I took a dinghy and sculled for nearly two hours, while the fresh perfumes, refined by gale and dew – the blackbird's listless note, with a freshness as if the dew were in it – the wings rising and falling in twinkling thickets – the vinous air of June, all dealt with me as they would. Hardly a thought or memory shaped itself. Nevertheless, I was conscious of that blest lucidity, that physical well-being of the brain 'like the head of a mountain in blue air and sunshine,' which is so rarely achieved except in youth. Thus in a prolongation of the mood of sleep, whose powerful touch was on me still, as I knew when I could find no answer for a questioning wayfarer, I covered several miles by one impulse, and as if nothing had intervened, resumed my breakfast thoughts. For the pebbles of a shallow had been shrieking under the boat, which could go no farther. Sounds and odours suddenly invaded and startled my senses. Solitude asserted itself. The day had come: and beads of night mist were humming as they fell upon the stream from off the willows.

Precisely there I had never been before, though I knew the river well. Drawn, however, by a clamour of poultry and brass pans, I presently found myself at a farmhouse door. The river was out of sight and even of hearing, for in summer it stole through the land like a dream.

HORAE SOLITARIAE

I wondered, also, if he remembered being at Stow-on-the-Wold only two years earlier, writing to his friend Gordon Bottomley on 12 March 1912:

Stow on the Wold is perfectly silent after a day of wind and rain, except the choir practising in the church over the way. It is a little stone town on a slope and summit of the Cotswolds and looks far away east over floods and red ploughlands.

Then Kingham, of which he said 'I know a lot about'. If he were here now would he be able to lead us to the old house where they stayed, strange but not unhappy, cobwebbed with shadows . . . that house with its long narrow dim drawing-room where a piano stood on a dais at one end and a ghost resided? I have not discovered it.

A surprising amount of letter-writing and visiting went on in Edward Thomas's life. Scarcely home from his week in Kingham and more plans are already afoot. On 19 May he tells Frost:

> I shall perhaps come soon. My wife and I are to have a week or so very probably early in July. We <u>have</u> to get in several calls. If we can we will come to Ledington. I assume there would be room (for 2 whole days).

And three days later he writes again to Bottomley:

> This is chiefly to ask you if you will be free early in July because Helen & I may very likely take a week's holiday then & come to you for part of the time – if you are free . . .

[NB: Bottomley's home is near Carnforth in Lancashire, a long way from Herefordshire!]

Robert Frost, *c.* 1915.

Gordon Bottomley, 1922.
(A drawing by John Nash)

But two days later he tells Bottomley he is

> reconsidering and it seems to me the best thing would be for me to come about June 13 for a week, or perhaps a little earlier, the 10th. Helen & I are to have such a little time together that we couldn't manage more than such a few days North that I thought this plan better, tho' it robs her of a very long desired pleasure. Now if I may come on the 10th or 13th may I do a morning's work? I get about so much now that if I don't work a little and everywhere I get behind. . . .

Five days later, 29 May, Thomas's mind is at last made up and

> I shall most likely come on the 13th and hope to find you recovered from Whitsun. But Helen can't come then & later on when we are together we shall have too little time, or that is what we should have done. . . .

Robert Frost is also eager for a visit soon. Edward Thomas, whom he would later call 'the only brother I ever had', was already far more in tune with him than the poets who lived close by in Herefordshire, Wilfrid Gibson and Lascelles Abercrombie.

Writing from Steep, on 6 June, Thomas told Frost that he was

> plagued with work, burning my candle at 3 ends . . . now for the same reason I can't come next week, not till about the 25th when we will both come . . . I have curtailed everything: am only just going up to Bottomley's to keep my promise and to work. So I shall be here until the 16th I expect — . . . I will let you know later what day exactly we shall come. I will not say We shall come but I feel we shall.

No wonder that Robert Frost confessed that one of his most popularly anthologised poems, 'The Road Not Taken', was 'a mild satire on the chronic vacillating habits of Edward Thomas'!

Throughout June and July 1914 there was a season of opera and ballet at Drury Lane that excited attention. Edward Thomas once told his friend Ian MacAlister that he found theatre plays extremely unreal. A lot of people talking and moving on a stage in front of an audience, did not appeal to him at all. Ballet and opera were more to his taste and he and Helen were among the crowds that flocked to Drury Lane for Mozart's *Magic Flute* and the acclaimed Diaghilev Ballet, visiting from Russia with its leading dancers, Karsavina and Nijinsky.

It is not only from Eleanor Farjeon's memoirs that we know that:

> Helen and Edward snatched an evening at the Ballet before they left for their days of walking which were to begin in Herefordshire, perhaps with a view to finding some holiday quarters for themselves near the Frosts.

ROYAL THEATRE, DRURY LANE

Sir Joseph BEECHAM'S

Grand Russian Season
JUNE-JULY 1914

Russian Opera & Russian Ballet

General Direction : SERGE DE DIAGHILEW
and Baron DIMITRI DE GUNZBOURG
Choreographic Director : MICHEL FOKINE

May

30 Saturday	Opera	Boris Godounov. Chaliapine Night

June

1 Monday	Opera	Boris Godounov. Chaliapine Night
2 Tuesday	Opera	Rosenkavalier.
3 Wednesday	Opera	Ivan le Terrible. Chaliapine Night
4 Thursday	Opera	Rosenkavalier.
5 Friday	Opera	Ivan le Terrible. Chaliapine Night
8 Monday	Opera	Prince Igor. Chaliapine Night
9 Tuesday		First Performance of the Ballet. *Daphnis and Chloé. Thamar. Scheherazade.
10 Wednesday	Opera	Boris Godounov. Chaliapine Night
11 Thursday	BALLET	*Papillons. Daphnis and Chloé. Petrouchka.
12 Friday	Opera	Prince Igor. Chaliapine Night
15 Monday	Opera-Ballet and Ballet	*Coq d'Or. Scheherazade.
16 Tuesday	BALLET	L'Oiseau de Feu. Papillons. Carnaval.
17 Wednesday	Opera	Prince Igor. Chaliapine Night
18 Thursday	Opera-Ballet and Ballet	*Le Rossignol. *Midas. Scheherazade.
19 Friday	Opera	Boris Godounov. Chaliapine Night
22 Monday	Opera	Prince Igor. Chaliapine Night
23 Tuesday	BALLET	*La Légende de Joseph. Thamar. Papillons. Strauss Night
24 Wednesday	Opera-Ballet and Ballet	Coq d'Or. Daphnis and Chloé.
25 Thursday	BALLET	Midas. La Légende de Joseph. Cléopâtre. Strauss Night
26 Friday	Opera-Ballet and Ballet	*Nuit de Mai. Petrouchka.
27 Saturday	Opera	Prince Igor. Chaliapine Night
29 Monday	Opera-Ballet and Ballet	Le Rossignol. Midas. La Légende de Joseph. Strauss Night
30 Tuesday	BALLET	Daphnis and Chloé. Cléopâtre. Le Spectre de la Rose.

July

1 Wednesday	Opera	La Khovantchina. Chaliapine Night
2 Thursday	Opera-Ballet and Ballet	Coq d'Or. Les Sylphides.
3 Friday	BALLET	Nuit de Mai. Oiseau de Feu.
4 Saturday	Opera	Dylan.
6 Monday	Opera	Ivan le Terrible. Chaliapine Night
7 Tuesday	BALLET	Midas. Le Lac des Cygnes. Petrouchka.
8 Wednesday	Opera-Ballet and Ballet	Nuit de Mai. Cléopâtre.
9 Thursday	Opera	Dylan.
10 Friday	Opera	La Khovantchina Chaliapine Night
11 Saturday	BALLET	Thamar. La Légende de Joseph. Papillons.
13 Monday	Opera-Ballet and Ballet	Nuit de Mai. Narcisse.
14 Tuesday	Opera-Ballet and Ballet	Le Rossignol. La Légende de Joseph. Les Sylphides.
15 Wednesday	Opera	Boris Godounov. Chaliapine Night
16 Thursday	BALLET	Carnaval. Le Lac des Cygnes. Le Spectre de la Rose.
17 Friday	Opera	Dylan.
18 Saturday	Opera-Ballet and Ballet	Coq d'Or. Scheherazade.
20 Monday	Opera	La Khovantchina. Petrouchka. Chaliapine Night
21 Tuesday	BALLET	Midas. La Légende de Joseph. Papillons.
22 Wednesday	Opera-Ballet and Ballet	Coq d'Or. Narcisse.
23 Thursday	Opera-Ballet and Ballet	Le Rossignol. Daphnis and Chloé. Scheherazade.
24 Friday	Opera	Boris Godounov. Chaliapine Night
25 Saturday	BALLET	Petrouchka. La Légende de Joseph. Papillons.

* First Performance in England.

General Manager : for Sir Joseph BEECHAM, Donald BAYLIS

From the souvenir programme, summer 1914, price 2/6.

Thomas himself wrote to Eleanor on 24 June from 13 Rusham Road, Balham, his parents' house:

> My dear Eleanor   We are just starting for Ledbury and are in a real hurry. Last night by the way we were at the ballet and one of the nicest things in that hot air was Joan Thornycroft who transpired. Also *Thamar, Papillons* and *Joseph* in that order. Now we will go on Tuesday next if you will. . . .

This is confirmed by Joan Thornycroft's diary for 1914, where the words 'Drury Lane 10 to 8' are pencilled against 23 June, and by the exquisitely lavish Jubilee programme found among her papers. The ballets for 23 June are advertised just as Thomas names them.

So . . . 24 June and 'We are just starting for Ledbury'. And imagination moves us away from London nightlife to Helen and Edward making their way across London from Balham to Paddington to catch their train – on a no. 36 bus perhaps, or on the Bakerloo Line, opened in 1906. Had they booked tickets in advance, or did they present themselves at the Paddington booking office on arrival? And what time was it? If we take 'Adlestrop' literally, then they went in time for an express train . . . and there <u>was</u> only one. The non-stop express train, Paddington to Worcester, first appeared on the timetable in July 1900 and in 1914 still boasted Down in 2 hours 15 minutes and Up in 2 hours 20. It was due to depart at 1.40 p.m. and to arrive at Worcester at 3.55 p.m.

At 3.14 p.m. the said train was due to slip a carriage at Kingham and, assuming it was on time, then the unscheduled stop at Adelstrop would have been at 3.18 p.m.

Ramon Willey, a young man researching all this twenty-four years ago, suggested that 'the driver forgot to "slip carriage" at Kingham and was forced to execute this duty at the next station along the line . . . at Adlestrop?' But a Mr T.P. Cooper of the British Transport Public Records Office dismissed this:

Eleanor Farjeon wearing the dress (17/6d in the summer sale) bought at Polunin's, the Russian shop in Bond Street, London, during the 1914 Diaghilev season at Drury Lane.

136 LONDON, OXFORD, EVESHAM, WORCESTER & MALVERN.

Passenger timetable for 1914. This does not show the 10.20 a.m. arriving Adlestrop at 12.46 prior to departure at 12.48 (which is, however, shown on the Service timetable). The 1.40 p.m. Express train is listed on the far right of the timetable.

A slip coach was a vehicle incorporating a special uncoupling device which allowed it to be detached from a train at speed; passengers travelling in it were therefore able to alight at stations at which the main train did not stop. There would therefore be no likelihood of the Kingham slip coach being detached at Adlestrop. . . .

[Little likelihood, intervened my own railway adviser.] Mr T.P. Cooper continues:

It does occur to me that there is very little likelihood of being able to ascertain the precise reason why Mr Thomas's train called at Adlestrop on 24th June 1914. In all probability the delay was caused by a trivial matter – perhaps the snapping of a signal wire or something of that nature – and no record would survive of this day to day occurrence!

From Edward Thomas's Field Note Book
(No. 75) for 23–7 June 1914.

Anyone sensible might simply leave matters there. However, it interested me that
Ramon Willey had correctly located the travel date as 24 June, and not 23rd (as
others have since).

Willey did not have access to Thomas's Field Note Books either, in which
Thomas recorded such detail and which I have found essential. Edward Thomas
carried a note-book always. On walks in the country, staying with friends, notes
were made, jottings and references documented for future use, although, on
occasion, he seemed to doubt their relevance. In 1909 he had written to Bottomley:

> I think I agree with your preferences – also in what you say of notebooks. . . .
> But I shall not burn them I expect. Only I shall certainly use them less and less
> as I get more of an eye for subjects. Among my bad habits was that of looking
> thro old note books more & more exclusively for the details of things conceived
> independently. Also I am casting for subjects which will compel me to depend
> simply upon what I am – memory included but in a due subsidiary place.

The Field Note Books, now in the Berg Collection of the New York Public Library,
include in No. 75 this entry:

> 24th
> a glorious day from 4.20 a.m & at 10 tiers above tiers of white cloud with
> dirtiest grey bars above the sea of slate and dull brick by Battersea Pk – then

at Oxford tiers of pure white with loose longer masses above and gaps of dark clear blue above haymaking and elms.

Then we stopped at Adlestrop, thro the willows cd be heard a chain of blackbirds songs at 12.45 & one thrush & no man seen, only a hiss of engine letting off steam.

Stopping outside Campden by banks of long grass willow herb & meadowsweet, extraordinary silence between the two periods of travel – looking out on grey dry stones between metals & the shiny metals & over it all the elms willows & long grass – one man clears his throat – a greater than rustic silence. No house in view Stop only for a minute till signal is up.

Now stop like this outside Colwall on 27th w thrush singing on hillside above on rd

24th–27th At Leadington with Frost in always hot weather.

Was the first part of this noted on 24 June, and the rest added later? Or was it all jotted down on 27th when the train stopped at Colwall after the Thomases had left the Frosts and were travelling towards friends in Coventry? '. . . a chain of blackbirds songs' at 12.45 seems clear but, if true, then the Thomases cannot have been on an express train at all.

Poring over Bradshaws and the GWR Service timetable (which I am assured is more reliable than the Customer one) with railway expert Chris Turner, the 10.20 a.m. stopping train from Paddington seemed a strong contender, scheduled to arrive at Adlestrop at 12.46 p.m., only one minute after those blackbirds were heard.

Although it is not essential to know which train Edward Thomas was on, whether Helen was with him, whether – as Ramon Willey discovered – the hissing of the steam was caused by an automatic escape from the safety valve, the quest continued.

Midsummer Day falls on 24 June, and is not a day one would expect Thomas to forget, although nine years before it had escaped him, as he told Bottomley:

I forgot that it was Midsummer Day this week – tho I was sentimental enough to remember that I must celebrate it a few days before. One nightingale sang for a minute as I walked to my cottage on Tuesday. It was the last. The cuckoo is almost silent. The year has passed; the spring has done without me; I have not had one good hour of standing still and forgetting time.

A favourite folk-song, and one included in his *Poems and Songs for the Open Air* was:

As I walked out one Midsummer morning
To view the fields, yes, and to take the air . . .

On Midsummer Day 1914 there was no walking – just a train journey. In late June 1974, when Ramon Willey visited Adlestrop with Thomas's daughters Bronwen and Myfanwy, they found, on the banks of both Down and Up lines of the disused railway cutting, different varieties of willow-herb and clusters of creamy, late blooming meadow sweet. These, as well as grasses, are linked together in a passage from Thomas's *The Heart of England*:

> When wind plays with the perfectly level surfaces of the grasses their colours close in and part and knit arabesques in the path of the light sand martens – nearer, and sometimes in the water, the branched meadow-sweet mingles the foam of its blossom and the profuse verdure of its leaves with willow-herb.

There may, today, be more of the Rosebay willow-herb, lover of old railway tracks and bombed sites, but in 1914 there was a profusion of the Great willow-herb, nicknamed Codlins-and-Cream, which grows well in watery damp places – the Evenlode runs behind the Down platform at Adlestrop. Writing about nearby Kingham's flowering plants in 1911, Warde Fowler found that the willow-herb overwhelmed even the purple loosestrife and he stressed:

> By willow-herb I mean, of course, the plant called 'codlins and cream', not the rose-bay willow-herb, which loves woods, though it is to be found close by the brook on the railway bank, blooming in September brilliantly, nor the smaller plants of the same genus, which add but little to the splendour of the stream. I suppose the very dry hot summer of 1911 exactly suited the constituents of the willow-herb, although I cannot explain why.

The summer of 1914 was equally warm and dry. There were two violent thunderstorms and one hailstorm recorded in the North Cotswolds, but the temperature in the shade of the stationmaster's house was exactly 80°F on 24 June; it was undoubtedly 'one afternoon of heat'.

In 1914 the row of willow trees at right angles with the Down line were already gnarled and pollarded, past their best, and forming a prominent part of the landscape. They remain today.

One most noticeable change between Thomas's view of 'Adlestrop' and that of today can surely be seen in the fields at harvest time; today's great cumbersome rolls of hay, often ominously cloaked in black plastic, could scarcely be described

> No whit less still and lonely fair
> Than the high cloudlets in the sky. . . .

James Harvey Woolliams, a descendant of farmer Will Woolliams, who farmed Fern Farm and later Lower Farm in Adlestrop, told me:

Farmer Will Woolliams of Lower Farm, Adlestrop,
c. 1905. Woolliams married Kate Holton of Hardwick
Farm, nr Banbury, in Banbury Parish Church in 1894.
He farmed Fern Farm, and latterly Lower Farm,
Adlestrop, and is probably the builder of the haycocks
in the poem.

I first became aware of 'Adlestrop' on my first day as a new boy, aged 10, at
Bloxham School. It was customary for the senior boys to cruise about asking,
'What is your name?' . . . 'Where do you live?', etc. The answer, 'Adlestrop',
caused an astonished pause, and then 'Yes I remember . . .'. It had been a set
poem the previous term! I heard it many times that day!

Not until older did I appreciate how evocative the poem was of the
countryside I knew. That the haycocks were in my Great Uncle's field didn't
enter my mind. The poem was in the same class as 'I wandered lonely as a
cloud . . .', so evocative of the daffodils I had seen beside the lake and beneath

the trees in Adlestrop park. I didn't connect the poem beyond my Adlestroponian vision of the English Countryside.

Much more recently, as my parents' generation has died off, and retirement has removed me (gratefully) from the 'rat race', I have become much more interested in my ancestors. While making a family tree and focussing on what individuals were like, I realised that my Great Uncle Will must have been farming Lower Farm at the time of Edward Thomas's famous stop, and mentioned in a footnote that he was probably the builder of the famous haycocks.

Woolliams ended with a very personal PS: 'Must try to visit Edward Thomas's grave in France, before I am buried . . . at Adlestrop.'

Among the various Adlestrop scenes, the station, the cottages, the wild flowers, in the thick red photograph album lovingly arranged by Ramon Willey in 1975 are two black and white postcards dating from the First World War. They are of the

Vimy railway station, *c.* 1900.

Vimy railway station, France, First World War. Haymaking is going on in the background.

railway station at Vimy, not far from Arras where Thomas died, and in the background, still and lonely, are French haycocks.

In his anthology *This England*, published in 1915, a book he wished to make 'as full of English character and country as an egg is of meat', Edward Thomas included two of his own poems under the pseudonym Edward Eastaway. One was 'Haymaking':

> In the field sloping down,
> Park-like to where its willows showed the brook
> Haymakers rested. . . .
> The men leaned on their rakes to begin,
> But still. And all were silent. . . .

As inevitable and timeless as the scene through the train window that he, and perhaps Helen, glimpsed.

Helen never wrote of this, but in the moving story of her marriage, *World Without End* she tells of another journey, on 4 August, the day war was declared, accompanied by her two daughters and a Russian schoolboy who was spending the holidays with them. Thomas and their son, Merfyn, had cycled on ahead to Oldfields, the house in Leadington, near the Frosts, that they had arranged to rent. Travelling from Hampshire to Ledbury proved complicated and arduous.

On 3 August 1963, forty-nine years later almost to the day, *The Times* published Helen's article 'Poets' Holiday in the Shadow of War'. She offers no suggestion that

Haymakers resting. (Gwendolen Raverat, 1932)

she had visited the countryside or met the Frosts before. But Thomas's Field Note Book entry shows: '24th–27th At Leadington with Frost in always hot weather'. And on 27 June Thomas had written to Bottomley:

We are just leaving Frosts and on way round towards home again. . . . On Tuesday we went to the Russian Ballet & heard Strauss's 'Joseph'. I suspect the music was not good. Anyhow I did not like it & the ballet itself was a failure. The story outline was not simple and significant enough for the dancers to do much with it. 'Papillon', founded on Schumann, was very charming – a Pierrot story of 1830. 'Thamar' I expect you know – an Eastern Carpet set to music. We hope to go again next Tuesday. We saw Rupert Brooke at Gibson's on Wednesday, browner & older & better looking after his tour. Yesterday we saw 4 Abercrombies!

Mme Thamar KARSAVINA
in 'PAPILLONS'

The dancer Tamara Karsavina in the ballet Edward and Helen
Thomas saw at Drury Lane on 23 June 1914.

That month of August, 'in the shadow of war', with Frosts, Thomases, Abercrombies and Gibsons within short distances of each other, has been written about over and over again. Helen Thomas wrote that 'no excitement of war disturbed the peace of that beautiful country with its wealth of choicest apples, pears and plums hanging red and golden and purple from the branches of innumerable fruit trees'. Eleanor Farjeon, who joined the Thomases in lodgings close by, crystallised the heightened time with her vivid account in *The Last Four Years*, culminating in the now famous Cider Supper, when she 'drank all the poets in Gloucestershire under the table'.

Wilfrid Gibson's nostalgic poem 'The Golden Room' also evokes a memorable period of place, mood and friendship. 'Do you remember that still summer evening? . . .' he wrote, in retrospect, in 1925, before listing a cast of poets and wives who may, or may not, have all been in his house, the Old Nailshop, at one time. He also says:

> 'Twas in July
> Of nineteen-fourteen that we sat and talked . . .

Wilfrid and Geraldine Gibson at their home, the Old Nail Shop, Greenway, Dymock.

but, looking at letters, diaries and dates, I don't think 'twas! It was much more likely to have been 24 June, the very same day as the Adlestrop incident, when we know that Frosts, Thomases and Brooke met together . . . or even an amalgamation of several occasions. Memory can play strange tricks.

When, for instance, Helen Thomas recorded 'Adlestrop' for the Argo Record Company on 8 April 1964, fifty years after the train journey, was a chord struck? Might she have thought to herself 'What _we_ saw was Adlestrop'? And, if she had, would it have changed the poem in any way? Is there no case for poetic licence? As Emily Tennyson told her sister in connection with Tennyson's 'Crossing The Bar': 'Alfred has told you there was no particular bar. It is curious how little credit people give to the imagination of a poet.'

By autumn 1914 the poets were separated and that winter Edward Thomas's letters were concerned with 'the stream of poetry that was now in flood' and his indecision as to whether to follow the Frosts to America when they returned, or to enlist. It would have been the latter had he not slipped on New Year's Day, spraining his ankle badly and becoming 'laid up quite immoveable'.

He started a new note-book for the New Year 1915, lying awkwardly on a sofa. An odd-looking book, printed in Germany; the page I have seen has an advertisement for a 'Continental Tennis Ball' and facing it, upside-down, some typical Edward Thomas jottings.

First of all: Train stopped within station at Adlestrop vi.14.

Next: Tratton mill 15 vi,14

And lastly: The stray bird la-la-la

All three are scratched out.

Was Thomas drawing on last summer's notes and six months later trying to make sense of them? The stray bird would, on 17 January feature in the poem 'The Unknown Bird'. Was Tratton Mill in any way linked to 'The Mill Pond', written on 18 January, an idea suggested during the Bottomley visit that June? I have found no clues. But 'Adlestrop' was written on 8 January, one of five poems written between 7 and 9 January.

Both R. George Thomas, in the notes to _Collected Poems_ (1978), and William Cooke, _Edward Thomas: A Critical Biography_ (1970), explore the background to the drafts, the revising of the poem, punctuation changes, proof-readings and possible inaccuracies.

'"Adlestrop" is unusual in that its first stanza went through four versions in the two manuscript drafts of the poem, which otherwise needed little correction before it was printed' wrote Cooke; and R. George Thomas mentions the 'punctuation variants as an example of Thomas's care over punctuation in most of his early poems':

~~Yes I remember Adlestrop,~~
~~At least the name. One afternoon~~
            ~~train~~
~~The express slowed down there & drew up~~
~~Quite~~

Yes, I remember Adlestrop,
At least the name. One afternoon
Of heat   The ~~steam~~ train slowed ~~down~~ & drew up
There unexpectedly. 'Twas June.

The steam hissed. Someone cleared his throat.
~~But no one left~~ No one left & no one came
On the bare platform. What I saw
Was Adlestrop, only the name,

And willows, willow herb & grass,
And meadowsweet. The haycocks dry
Were not less still & lonely fair
Than the high cloud tiers in the sky.

And all that minute a blackbird sang
Close by, and round him, mistier,
Farther & farther ~~off~~, all the birds
Of Oxfordshire & Gloucestershire.

                                        (1st draft)

Yes, I remember Adlestrop—
At least the name. One afternoon
        the express train
Of heat ~~the train slowed &~~ drew up there
    Against its custom.
~~There unexpectedly.~~ It '~~T~~was June.

Yes, I remember Adlestrop—
The name, because
~~At least the name.~~ One afternoon
Of heat, the express train drew up there
~~Against the custom~~
Unwontedly. It was late June.

The steam hissed. Someone cleared his throat.
No one left & no one came
On the bare platform. What I saw
Was Adlestrop, only the name,

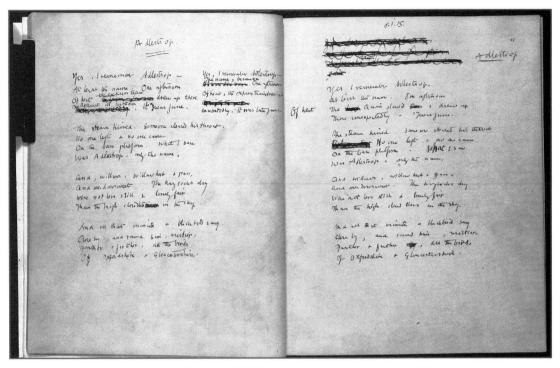

The original draft pages of 'Adlestrop', now held in the British Library.

And, willows, willow herb & grass,
And meadowsweet. The haycocks dry
Were not less still & lonely fair
Than the high cloudlets ~~tiers~~ in the sky.

And all that minute a blackbird sang
Close by, and round him, mistier,
Farther & farther, all the birds
Of Oxfordshire & Gloucestershire.

(2nd draft)

Preparing his own poems for publication under his pseudonym, after enlisting but before going out to France, Thomas finally put a full stop after the word 'Yes' at the start of the poem. Many editors since, R. George Thomas included, prefer the comma. Today both versions can be found in anthologies. A minor detail perhaps? Not entirely. The comma seems to allow a moment's reflection; the full stop is more positive. The punctuation particularly affects the speaking aloud of the poem.

The critic John Bayley accepts Thomas's full stop, and writes:

The pattern of speech dismisses the rural charm of the name (which has made it so much remembered in anthologies) almost instantly. The name is put to one side by the oncoming experience, in the same way that the poet himself, and his speech, will be, in the last stanza, emphasised in Thomas's first and second drafts by the phrase 'At least the name'. In becoming simply 'the name', Adlestrop adds to the indefinably memorable and yet casual nature of what occurs there. What happened has too the deepest sadness of things in it, a fact which must very likely have been noted by Walter de la Mare, some of whose own best poems give the same impression, though without any of the same peculiar accuracy, an accuracy which is both comforting and desolating. De la Mare, like Thomas, was not at home in a world which both saw with such subdued intensity. The strange sadness of the poem goes with the comedy of its name. . . . that much anthologised poem does tell us a lot about Thomas. It is indeed, in its own peculiar sense, about Thomas.

The year 1997 was the eightieth anniversary of Edward Thomas's death and the Imperial War Museum commemorated this with a facsimile edition of *Poems 1917*. In her introduction, Myfanwy Thomas, the poet's daughter, said:

Sadly, although he had carefully selected and arranged the 64 poems, he did not see proofs: the book was published six months after his death at the opening of the Battle of Arras on 9th April, 1917. I have of course seen and carefully handled the original volume – but only, as it were, as something precious. I have never before studied the contents or the order in which the poems are arranged. This was because when I became interested in reading and studying the poems, the collected edition had already appeared and the rare copy of the 1917 *Poems* was something to be handled delicately – not one to be carried about or packed in holiday luggage.

And secondly, the first thing to be done with any selection or anthology of poems is to search through the index and then to be disappointed to find many favourites are missing. I was glad to see he had included 'As the team's head brass', 'In Memoriam', the family poems to Mother, Merfyn, Bronwen and me (though as a child I resented his perpetuating my spectacles and straight hair!) but where was 'Old Man' in which my small self was the proud villain, and where too was 'The Brook' in which I was the wise philosopher? I found 'Swedes' and 'Cockcrow' with all their exotic colour, and the lovely 'Words' he had placed last of all. And 'Adlestrop' made the first of its many many appearances in selections and anthologies.

I remember, as a schoolgirl, feeling resentful when our English teacher dissected a poem, pulled it apart, probed and questioned. 'It's the poem that matters', I thought. And, despite this detection work on Adlestrop, I still believe that. I am only too aware that many will feel as Susan Hill does and describes in her book *The Spirit of the Cotswolds*. Having driven through Oddington and heading towards Chipping Norton, 'locally always known as Chippy' on the main A436 that leads from Stow-on-the-Wold, she tells us that she sees a sign:

Familiar perhaps. Adlestrop. Adlestrop? I feel a stir of affection when I read or hear the name, as if it were that of an old friend and it brings with it a whole train of associations in its wake, echoes of English poets and poetry and of nostalgia for the peace of remote rural villages half a century ago. One of the finest twentieth-century English poets and celebrants of the countryside, Edward Thomas, is best known for this one poem – 'Adlestrop'.

I learned it when I was at school and I still know it by heart and when I pass the signpost pointing to Adlestrop, the opening stanzas begin to wind through my head. I am told that when they closed Adlestrop Station, they took down the sign Edward Thomas saw and put it up in the bus shelter, but I have never actually seen it because I have never been to Adlestrop and I don't want to go. The magic of the name and the beauty of the poem might be spoiled. I like to think that Adlestrop isn't a *real* place at all. So the signpost off the road points in a direction I shall never take.

Stanley Herbert

Do You Remember Adlestrop?

NORMAN NICHOLSON

Someone, somewhere, must have asked that question – Robert
Frost, may be, or Abercrombie, or, that now
Forgotten genius, John W. Haines, who scarcely
Wrote a line himself but knew the knack
Of making others write them. Someone
Who called at Steep that cold January, '15,
The poet laid up in bed with a sprained ankle – and 'Yes,
Yes, Yes!' he shouted, as the happy accident
Unsnecked the trapdoor of his memory,
'And willows, willow-herb, and grass'
Burgeoned from a compost of fermenting words –
'Yes, Yes, Yes!' and now everyone remembers.

Is there no question
To fork air into my long-dormant root-stock? No
Fag-card flash of a boy's bright slagbank day,
The wild barley in the back street, the quite impossible catch
That snatched the match and the cup? The questions come,
Blunt and bullying as a bad conscience,
But always the wrong ones. – 'Do you remember
Stoke Newington, Stockport, Crewe or Solihull?' –
And sadly, guiltily, I reply: 'I'm sorry' –
The trapdoor banged down tight, the compost sour and black –
'No' –
Not even sure if I've ever been there –
'No. I don't remember.'

1981

Actually Adlestrop?

(Homage to Edward Thomas)

MONICA HOYER

The sudden halt; the hissing steam;
did Edward Thomas only dream
that unexpected incident?
Or was it truly heaven-sent?

1993

Bernard Brett

Not Adlestrop

(*Homage to Edward Thomas*)

MICHAEL HOROVITZ

No, I don't remember Adlestrop
(Moreton-in-Marsh's the nearest stop)

But when I was small there were puffer trains
Cresting bridges that wound over leafy lanes

And one that stopped at a long white gate
To let a herd of cows pass, late

One summer evening at a level crossing
In the Cotswold hamlet of Little Bossing

1994

Names

JULIAN ENNIS

When we clanked through Adlestrop,
Only the station, I remembered
The name, and thought again of the tormented poet
Who had lodged it among our myths, a word
For keeping, and of his counties
And his birds, and the guns.

And when I read about the red, red rose,
How can I not smell the constant sweet
Scent, and know what my lost love was like?

So deep within us the writing sinks.
We become its hosts, it breeds in us;
The names stalk us on our journey,
Lurking on platforms where flowers,
Red forget-me-nots,
Stand guard in tubs.

Adlestrop – Only the Name

ANNE HARVEY

Edward Thomas is known for his love of place-names. They appear frequently in his prose and poetry. Some of those most often recalled belong to the poems he wrote for his children. For Bronwen, his elder daughter, he decides:

> If I should ever by chance grow rich
> I'll buy Codham, Cockridden and Childerditch,
> Roses, Pyrgo, and Lapwater. . . .

For his son, Merfyn, he writes:

> If I were to own this countryside
> As far as a man in a day could ride
> And the Tyes were mine for giving or letting, . . .
> Wingle Tye and Margaretting
> Tye, — and Skreens, Gooshays, and Cockerells,
> Shellow, Rochetts, Bandish and Pickerells,
> Martins, Lambkins and Lilliputs
> Their copses, ponds, roads, and ruts. . . .
> I would give them all to my son
> If he would let me have any one
> For a song, a blackbird's song, at dawn.

And, lastly, for Myfanwy:

> What shall I give my daughter the younger
> More than will keep her from cold and hunger?
> I shall not give her anything. . . .

But, finally, he leaves her 'Steep and her own world' – perhaps the most important of all the places he lived in or visited. The Thomas family moved from their Hampshire home at Wick Green for another in nearby Steep in 1913. He wrote to Eleanor Farjeon on 21 July: 'Steep on Tuesday, and for all I know for ever after.'

It was this writer friend who typed out the poems, along with others, for the children and who, more than anyone, shared his fascination for place-names. She herself wrote *Nursery Rhymes of London Town* – verses that gave twisted double

Helen and Myfanwy (aged three) in 1913. Merfyn (thirteen) is in the background, with toothache.

meanings to King's Cross, Wormwood Scrubs, Shepherd's Bush and so on – as well as a *Sussex Alphabet*. One cannot doubt Edward Thomas's influence in her lines:

> From Victoria I can go
> To Pevensey Level and Piddinghoe,
> Open Winkins and Didling Hill,
> Three Cups Corner and Selsey Bill. . . .

The poet and critic Leslie Norris, writing on Thomas's use of 'place-name' poems for his children, observes that they also:

> contain lines which are clear evidence of Thomas's most careful and delicious observation, lines full of solid re-creation:
>
> > Fields where plough-horses steam and plovers
> > Fling and whisper
>
> It is in such lines that we must look for Thomas's sense of place, in such particularity, in his expression of minute detail. For him actual places are not named, but are identified by a group of trees, a snail, a white stone. 'Adlestrop', the name, is an accident. He remembers it
>
> > . . . because one afternoon
> > Of heat the express-train drew up there
> > Unwontedly

and the word is less important than the 'willows, willow-herb, and grass' which grew there. And when Thomas wants, in this poem, to express enormous distance, an impression of infinite skies fading out of sight, he does it by using place-names. When he names Oxfordshire and Gloucestershire, it is not to name a defined geographical region, but to suggest an unending extension of space.

> And for that minute a blackbird sang
> Close by, and round him, mistier,
> Farther and farther, all the birds
> Of Oxfordshire and Gloucestershire.

That whole verse is, in fact, an interesting paradoxically successful feat. The poet, through the repeated and deepening use of those feminine rhymes – mistier, farther, farther, Oxfordshire, Gloucestershire – transforms those solid counties into visionary and tangible places, made of fading birdsong. . . .

A wood engraving by Linda Holmes (1999) to illustrate 'Adlestrop' for the second set of notecards published by the Edward Thomas Fellowship.

The name, Adlestrop, glimpsed from the train, would have intrigued Thomas, and here I must mention some controversy over the pronunciation. A small contingency plump for the long 'Ay' sound as in ladle, table, cradle. Certainly a fine teacher of my acquaintance taught her pupils to speak it like this. We will never know how Thomas himself spoke it, but the short 'a' is generally accepted.

Whichever you choose, the letter A stands for Adlestrop and in Volume 38 of The English Place-name Society the village comes first in the listing for the area of Gloucestershire known as 'Slaughter Hundred'. It is part of the upper division lying north of the lower division and occupies the hilly country between the Rivers Evenlode and Dikler. Its centre is Stow-on-the-Wold.

'Adlestrop – only the name' wrote Edward Thomas, perhaps with an inkling, as it was the sort of thought that would cross his mind, that such a name would have a history. Topography scholars could spend hours on the subject, and add to my findings. The name has changed and fluctuated since Saxon times and appears variously over the centuries as:

> Titlestrop 714; Tedestrop 1086; Tattlest(h)rop 1291; Tattlestrop 1292; Tatelesthorp(e) 1338; Tatilstrope *c*. 1603; Tetlestropt 1221; Thatlestrope and Thetillestroppe; Tadelecthorpe (sic) 1287; Tadelest(h)rop 1298; Tadlestrop 1334; Tadilthorp 1577; Attlesthorpe 1330; Athilthorp(e) 1535; Addlestroppe 1627; Athilthroppe 1597; Edelstrop 1599; Adelsthrope/Adelsthorpe/ Tatelsthrope 1626, Ad(d)lestrop 1684.

The entry in the Place-name Society publication suggests that:

> In view of the early spellings with the initial T – there can be little doubt that the original form of the name was Tat(e)les-thorp; the latter form Attle-, Adle-, etc. arises from wrong analysis of phrases like 'at Tatlesthrop' . . . i.e. Taetel's dependent farmstead – although the O.E. personal name Taetel is not on record, unless the name of a Mercian money dealer, Tatel is a variant of it and occurs in place-names such as Tetilles wode, Talton (9 miles north of Adlestrop) and Tatsfield.

Some vocabulary usage of earlier times seems centred in specific areas. Throp, meaning 'secondary settlement', occurs chiefly in the south Cotswolds, although Adlestrop is one example found further north in the Evenlode valley.

Writing in the magazine *ARCHIV* (London) in 1980, John Adlard, an astute literary detective, refers to Edward Thomas's editing of *Words & Places* by Isaac Taylor, in 1911. He quotes Taylor:

> Wars may trample down or extirpate whatever grows upon soil, excepting its wild flowers and the names of those sites upon which man has found a home . . . a useful test-word is *thorpe*, *throp* or *trop* . . . it means an aggregation of men or houses . . . a village. But what does Thomas make of *thorpe*, *throp* and *trop*?

> Yes. I remember Adlestrop —
> The name, . . .

There is no attempt to interpret the name; its queerness, its mystery are left with us, and ordinary people who know few poems know this particular Cotswold place and give it a special significance because of sixteen lines of verse by Edward Thomas.

Adlestrop – only the name?

Applestrop

DOUGLAS VERRALL

No. I've forgotten Applestrop –
Was that the name? One afternoon – or morning –
Rain belting under a cloudless sky, the train lurched
Uncomfortably. Sometime in July, perhaps.

I do remember coughing. Or did I sneeze
When the driver hissed impatiently
Waiting for some poet to appear,
To note the station name – or buy a platform ticket?

And dandelions, daisies overgrown
In lovers' grass and lupins dying witless
In the golden sun looked forlornly lonely
In the balmy breeze for no one came

Until at last a rabbit,
Bouncing into view, signalled to
All his distant cousins who misty-eyed went
Romping through the fields of Gloucestershire. Or Gwent.

1998

'Adlestrop'. (A wood engraving by John O'Connor)

A Literary Pilgrim

ANNE HARVEY

Writing about William Cobbett in *A Literary Pilgrim in England* in 1917 Edward Thomas said: 'That he loved travel is clear.' Then, quoting Cobbett: 'There is no pleasure in travelling except on horseback or on foot. Carriages take your body from place to place, and if you merely want to be conveyed they are very good; but they enable you to see and to know nothing at all of the country.'

Edward Thomas probably travelled the length and breadth of the country more than any other poet of his time or since. The age of carriages was over and although in 1908 he told Gordon Bottomley 'Cycling I hate' this must have been a momentary grumble; he cycled a tremendous amount, often accompanied by his son, Merfyn. Walking was his favourite means of travel and he is said to have covered most of southern England on foot. A much loved image of him is the lithoprint showing him as a walker, knapsack on back, by the fifteen-year-old Robin Guthrie.

Eleanor Farjeon wrote:

> To walk with Edward Thomas in any countryside was to see, hear, smell and know it with fresh senses. . . . You would not walk that road again as you did before. You would know it in a new way.
>
> He himself was difficult to know. He was a man of moods, and whether he was happy or melancholy he withheld himself. While he shared with you his knowledge of the things that meant most to him, his self-knowledge was what he did not share. He reserved this as a deep pool hides a secret under the surface that reflects clearly every image and movement passing over it. To go for a walk with Edward Thomas was a sure way of discovering something you hadn't noticed about a tree, a weed, a flower, some difference in the sweet or acid notes in birds, how dry earth smells in spring, crumbles darkly in autumn, its freckled look under thaw, the feel of the sun on a stone or on your skin, the weather's changes of mood all the year round.

Thomas's brother, Theodore, recalled:

> On his best days Edward was a good companion by reason of his immense knowledge of all one can see or hear on a country walk, and his easy and mellifluous way of putting over such knowledge. On his worst days the onus was upon you to originate conversation if you wanted it. Even in these moods he was easily stirred by the song of a human or a bird. . . .

Many of Thomas's poems spring from what he saw on his walks, 'Adlestrop' is the only example of a poem inspired by what was seen on a train journey. Although his father wrote of him 'After leaving Oxford he lived in English villages as far as he could get from any railway', he quite often took a train for those weekly trips from Hampshire to London to meet literary friends at St George's Restaurant in St Martin's Lane. His correspondence shows some knowledge of country stations, junctions and time-tables.

Journeys occur in certain essays. William Cooke, in his *Critical Biography*, suggests that a starting point for 'Adlestrop' was this excerpt from Thomas's essay 'England', published after his death:

A writer in *The Times* on patriotic poetry said a good thing lately: 'There may be pleasanter places, there is no *word* like home.' A man may have this feeling even in a far quarter of England. One man said to me that he felt it, that he felt England very strongly, one evening at Stogumber under the Quantocks. His train stopped at the station which was quite silent, and only an old man got in, bent, gnarled, and gross, a Caliban; 'but somehow he fitted in with the darkness and the quietness and the smell of burning wood, and it was all something I loved being part of.' We feel it in war-time or coming from abroad, though we may be far from home: the whole land is suddenly home.

Edward Thomas, 1917. (Lino-cut by Robin Guthrie, aged fifteen)

'This feeling', writes Cooke, 'was the inspiration for three poems, "Adlestrop", "Home" and "Good-night", which are, in his [Thomas's] own phrase, "inevitably English".'

Harry Coombes, in his 1956 *Critical Study*, draws attention to Edward Thomas's prose sketch 'A Third-class Carriage', where the scene is a train. He finds it interesting:

> because it shows the attitude and feeling, the values, that we associate with Thomas; it is also, in itself, clear in intention, forceful, unrepetitive, and vivid. . . . Thomas neatly and firmly communicates his sense of the indifference and insentience that develop in convention-ridden lives; the colonel, despite his pipe, and the youth, despite his golf-clubs, cannot because of their snobbery live 'in the now'. And they are not simply two persons in a railway carriage; they represent a way of life that Thomas sees as not only limited and unpleasant but also, we feel, as a disastrous development: to them, the only thing that may commend the small English town or village - - - 'it's not much of a place' - - - is the railway works.

Harry Coombes does not mention this in association with 'Adlestrop' but William Cooke confirms my own feelings that this prose sketch, published posthumously in 1928, contains 'a similar situation as that evoked in the poem'.

A Third-class Carriage

EDWARD THOMAS

When the five silent travellers saw the colonel coming into their compartment, all but the little girl looked about in alarm to make sure that it was a mere third-class carriage. His expression, which actually meant a doubt, whether it was not perhaps a fourth-class carriage, had deceived them; and one by one – some with hypocritical, delaying mock-unconsciousness, others with faint meaning looks – they began to look straight before them again, except while they cast casual eyes on the groups waving or turning away from the departing train. Even then every one looked round suddenly because the colonel knocked the ashes out of his pipe with four sharp strokes on the seat. He himself was looking neither to the right nor to the left. But he was not, therefore, looking up or down or in front of him; he was restraining his eyes from exercise, well knowing that nothing worthy of them was within range. The country outside was ordinary downland, the people beside him were but human beings.

Impression of a GWR train with 'Saint' class of locomotive, London to Worcester, 1914.
(Neville Morris)

Having knocked out the ashes, he used his eyes. He was admiring the pipe –
without animation, even sternly – but undoubtedly admiring what he and the
nature of things had made of the briar in 1910 and 1911. It had been choice from
the beginning, not too big, not too small, neither too long nor too short, neither
heavy nor slim; absolutely straight, in no way fanciful, not pretentious; the grain of
the wood uniform – a freckled or 'bird's-eye' grain – all over. In his eyes it was
faultless, yet not austerely perfect; for it won his affection as well as his admiration
by its 'cobby' quality, inclining to be shorter and thicker than the perfect one which
he had never yet possessed save in dreams. A woman who by unprompted
intelligence saw the merit of this favourite could have done anything with the
colonel; but no woman ever did, though when instructed by him they all assented in
undiscriminating warmth produced by indifference to the pipe and veneration for
its master. As for the men, he had chosen his friends too well for there to be one
among them who could not appreciate the beauty of the pipe, the exquisitely
trained understanding of the colonel.

He was not merely its purchaser; in fact, it was not yet paid for. The two years of
expectant respect, developing into esteem, cordial admiration, complacent
satisfaction, had not been a period of indolent possession. Never once had he failed
in alert regard for the little briar, never overheated it, never omitted to let it rest

when smoked out, never dropped it or left it about among the profane, never put into it any but the tobacco which now, after many years, he thought the best, the only, mixture. Its dark chestnut with an amber overgleam was reward enough.

As he filled the pipe he allowed his eyes to alight on it with a kindliness well on this side of discretion, yet unmistakable once the narrow but subtle range of his emotional displays had been gauged. He showed no haste as he kept his pale, short second finger working by a fine blend of instinct and of culture; his whole body and spirit had for the time being committed themselves to that second finger-tip. After having folded the old but well-cared-for pouch, removed the last speck of tobacco from his hands, and restored the pipe to his teeth, he lit a wooden match slowly and unerringly, and sucked with decreasing force until the weed was deeply, evenly afire. The hand holding the match, the muscles of the face working, the eyes blinking slightly, the neck bending – all seemed made by divine providence for the pipe.

When the match was thrown out of the window, and the first perfect smoke-cloud floated about the compartment, only the eye that sees not and the nose that smells not could deny that it was worth while. The dry, bittersweet aroma – the perfumed soul of brindled tawniness – was entirely worthy of the pipe. No wonder that the man had consecrated himself to this service. To preserve and advance that gleam on the briar, to keep burning that Arabian sweetness, was hardly less than a vestal ministry.

There was not a sound in the carriage except the colonel's husky, mellow breathing. His grey face wrinkled by its office, his stiff white moustache of hairs like quills, his quiet eyes, his black billycock hat, his unoccupied recumbent hands, the white waterproof on which they lay, his spotless brown shoes matching the pipe, were parts of the delicate engine fashioning this aroma. Certainly they performed no other labour. His limbs moved not; his eyes did not see the men and women or the child, or the basketful of wild roses in her lap, which she looked at when she was not staring out at the long, straight-backed green hill in full sunlight, the junipers dappling the steep slope, and whatever was visible to her amongst them. His brain subdued itself lest by its working it should modify the joys of palate and nostrils.

At the next station a pink youth in a white waterproof, brown shoes, and hollycock hat, carrying golf-clubs and a suit-case, entered the carriage. The colonel noted the fact, and continued smoking. Not long afterwards the train stopped at the edge of a wood where a thrush was singing, calling out very loud, clear things in his language over and over again. In this pause the other passengers were temporarily not content to look at the colonel and speculate on the cost of his tobacco, his white waterproof, and his teeth and gold plate, on how his wife was dressed, whether any of his daughters had run away from him, why he travelled third-class; they looked out of the window and even spoke shyly about the thrush, the reason of the stop, their destination. Suddenly, when all was silent, the little girl held up her roses towards the colonel saying:

'Smell.'

Illustration © 1998 Paul Howard from *Classic Poetry*. (Reproduced by permission of the publisher, Walker Books Ltd, London)

The colonel, who was beginning to realize that he was more than half-way through his pipe, made an indescribable joyless gesture designed to persuade the child that he was really delighted with the suggestion, although he said nothing, and did nothing else to prove it. No relative or friend was with her, so again she said:

'Smell. I mean it, really.'

Fortunately, at this moment the colonel's eyes fell on the pink youth, and he said:

'Is Borely much of a place, sir?'

Every one was listening.

'No, sir; I don't think so. The railway works are there, but nothing else, I believe.'

'I thought so,' said the colonel, replacing his pipe in his mouth and his mind in its repose. Every one was satisfied. The train whistled, frightening the thrush, and moved on again. Until it came to the end of the journey the only sound in the carriage was the colonel knocking out the ashes of his pipe with a sigh.

Adlestrop

B.S. BEEZER

A train's enforced delay
At a country station
For about a minute
On a summer's day,
   Is but a little thing;
Birds singing far away
With a blackbird very near
And a poet noticing
The station's name,
   Are only little things;
But from such littleness
Does Adlestrop today
Remember Edward Thomas
And his belated fame:
   And that's no little thing.

The Poem and the Place

SEAN STREET

Our response to environment, that which we often refer to as 'a sense of Place' is a complex thing. On the one hand, as V.S. Naipaul wrote in *The Enigma of Arrival*:

> Land is not land alone, something that simply is itself. Land partakes of what we breathe into it, is touched by our moods and memories.

On the other hand those moods and memories can be shaped by events, sometimes provoking an emotional answer linked to the physical identity of the place, changed and charged by circumstance. It can be a very personal thing – a memory of a summer evening's walk by a river for example. It can be a happening of national or international significance – an aircraft crashes on a small town or a mining disaster engulfs a village. Whatever it is, how can those places ever be the same again? How can Aberfan be now the Welsh mining town it wanted all along to be? People make places, but events make them too. The pause in Edward Thomas's train journey was an event. It was an event which focused itself on a sense of Place, and the evocation of Thomas's response to the emerging significance of Time and Place has been mirrored, years later, in Brian Patten's poem about Lockerbie.

Lockerbie

BRIAN PATTEN

Yes, I remember the place –
The station. One dull afternoon
The train drew up there
Unexpectedly.

Before the town was reached
From the windows I saw
The usual picture-postcard scenery.
The sheep-cropped fields revealed

No hint of catastrophe.
A few passengers looked up,
And jolted from a Sunday doze
They saw the place's name and froze.

Opposite me a woman wept.
Some people came aboard,
And passed on the baton of their grief
To those who left. The place's name

Was not observed by all.
Noses stuck in books some read on
As car parks, new housing, dull fields,
Were quickly passed, then gone.

Even if we never visit the scene ourselves, the pattern of letters that make its name is suddenly imbued with a new layer of meaning, and the place can never be the same again.

There is no evidence that Edward Thomas ever succumbed to the temptation to go back to Adlestrop and explore the place behind the name. Nevertheless his poem has changed the village's relationship with the world; poems of place are events in themselves, and the fact of their existence, of our knowing them, means that we are changed in our view of their subject, whatever it may be. The image of the place is filtered through the perception that originally caught the essence in words. Stand on Westminster Bridge in the early morning and try not to think of Wordsworth:

> This City now doth like a garment wear
> The beauty of the morning; silent, bare,
> Ships, towers, domes, theatres and temples lie
> Open unto the fields, and to the sky;
> All bright and glittering in the smokeless air . . .

Inevitably we must seek comparisons: how has it changed, how does it remain the same? There can occasionally come even now a quality of light to make us feel 'this is what he meant'. We may play with the fancy as to where he was standing at the moment the poem was conceived, may attempt to put ourselves almost literally in his situation and so on.

That is something else a poem of place does, because it is not simply about the place, but the poet IN the place. Thus we find ourselves standing beside Wordsworth, linked across time by the continuing presence of the subject of his sonnet around us. In the same way how can we walk on Beeny Cliff in Cornwall and not see the ghost of early love as Thomas Hardy saw it when he wrote:

> What if still in chasmal beauty looms that wild weird western shore,
> The woman now is – elsewhere – whom the ambling pony bore,
> And nor knows nor cares for Beeny, and will laugh there nevermore.

Likewise standing on Canute's Tower at St Beuno's in Wales, we cannot help but scan the skies for a glimpse of Gerard Manley Hopkins's Windhover:

> I caught this morning morning's minion, king-
> dom of daylight's dauphin, dapple-dawn-drawn Falcon, in his riding
> Of the rolling level underneath him steady air . . .

It is not necessary of course to go to the place to enjoy the poem. We can read Gray's words born in Stoke Poges Churchyard and see in our mind's eye archetypal images of the time, as if perhaps in a Caspar David Friedrich painting:

> The Curfew tolls the knell of parting day,
> The lowing herd wind slowly o'er the lea,
> The plowman homeward plods his weary way,
> And leaves the world to darkness and to me.

Nevertheless how often do we find ourselves moved to make a pilgrimage to a spot on the map which otherwise would have had no significance in our lives, but for the poem it inspired? Much literary tourism has resulted from this impulse. By giving us the picture of a church clock eternally at ten to three Rupert Brooke has planted in us the expectation that to visit Grantchester must be to enter an idyll outside of a world of rain and icy winds, where there is always honey for tea on a warm dream-England sunlit lawn. For many visitors it is hard to imagine the place in any other way than as it is painted in his famous poem. Sometimes that literary tourism can be more revealing than we might anticipate. I remember walking the hills above Henry Vaughan's home, Newton Farm at Llansantffraed, with the poet Anne Cluysenaar. As we climbed, Anne told me of a discovery she had recently made that perhaps could change the way we read Vaughan. In his poem 'Vanity of Spirit' he speaks of stones inscribed with 'hieroglyphics':

> Here of this mighty spring, I found some drills,
> With echoes beaten from the eternal hills;
>> Weak beams, and fires flashed to my sight,
>> Like a young east, or moon-shine night,
>> Which showed me in a nook cast by
>> A piece of much antiquity,
>> With hieroglyphics quite dismembered
>> And broken letters scarce remembered.
> I took them up, and (much joyed) went about
> T'unite those pieces, hoping to find out
> The mystery . . .

Is this a metaphysical conceit, or is he talking about something physically real here? Is it a metaphor? Our visit to this place seemed to provide an answer. Anne took me to a gully – dried up now but once a tributary of a brook that ran down past the farm. There we saw some stones, broken but clearly carrying deeply carved shapes – strange shapes – *hieroglyphics*. Were these Vaughan's stones from 'Vanity of Spirit'? Had we stumbled upon the physical inspiration of a great poem? If so it was walking in Vaughan's footsteps that opened the door.

It is possible to experience a poem – or a poet's entire *oeuvre* – on a number of levels. Take John Clare for example. In 'The Village Minstrel' written in 1821 at Helpston, the village of his birth, we read:

> While learned poets rush to bold extremes,
> And sunbeams snatch to light the muse's fires,
> An humble rustic hums his lowly dreams,
> Far in the swale where poverty retires . . .

Long before I went to Clare's countryside, I sensed that there was something one might almost call *fractured* about certain elements of him – a duality. There was of course the duality of his time, hung across two centuries. There was likewise the duality of his social situation, ripped by fashion as he was away from his natural world and then abandoned when the fad was for something else, leaving him stranded as a farmer in London and a man of letters in his own fields. There was also the double nature of his realities: his world revolved around two women, one real, his wife Martha, and the other, Mary Joyce, the childhood sweetheart whose ghost haunted him ever after.

And then I went to Helpston, and I saw the fracture in the very landscape. Come to the village as I did first, from the direction of Northampton, and you encounter an attractive, leafy, undulating countryside, peopled by welcoming villages and winding lanes. Arrive in Helpston and turn right . . . and within yards you are in the Fen, with the space limitless in all directions and the sun 'hung on nothing' in Clare's words. Everything is open, straight, spare, huge. The contrast in the turning of a corner could not be greater or more breathtaking, and it explains so much; even Clare's PLACE is on a hinge!

Birtley Aris

So we may see that the relationship between the poet and the place works in two ways. There are places that *form* the poet over a period of time. There are also places that *happen* to the poet – unexpected physical and emotional events which are caught in the poem's frame, then developed and shaped into events that in their turn happen to the *place*, giving it an essence that is finally formed in the response of the reader.

The exciting thing about the relationship between a person and a place is that we can all of us – poets or not – catch the spiritual spark that ignites when mood, location and situation touch in some sort of electric confluence. It happened for Edward Thomas in the summer of 1914 when a strange name on a station platform caused him to look up and catch the heat and stillness of a place which was for him at that moment without any context at all. And that is why WE remember Adlestrop.

In the end the place becomes something more than itself. In his poem 'Landscape and I', Norman MacCaig writes of a beloved mountain, Schiehallion, as seen across the waters of Loch Rannoch. For him it is 'more than mountain': by its very existence it instils 'a meaning, an idea'. We all have the capacity in us to experience this relationship with a location, whether it be rural, urban, a familiar environment, or a place that suddenly takes us by surprise, in the way a deep friendship begins. As MacCaig says:

> Oh,
> There's a Schielhallion anywhere you go.
> The thing is, climb it.

Vadstena

FRANCIS BERRY

Adlestrop was in my mind for about three months before I wrote 'Vadstena'. I approached Vadstena, coming from the West, on a ship called the *Venus* on the Gota Canal from Gothenberg to Stockholm. The scream from an inmate was unexpected. I suppose Adlestrop, coming from the East, was a surprise for Thomas and all the birds singing. I visited Adlestrop coming by bus (it was after Beeching) and was delighted to find the railway station name mounted in the village. . . . I was introduced to Edward Thomas by L.C. Knights of 'Scrutiny'. He read 'Adlestrop' to me I remember. . . .

> Yes, I remember the name,
> Vadstena; on that afternoon
> The steamer drew up beside the quay,
> Below the castle. It was July.
>
> I disembarked. And everywhere and everywhere
> There were roses, roses, roses, here
> Upon the castle and on the convent stone,
> And roses in the gardens of the wooden
>
> Houses. St Bridget's *kloster*.
>   And then the scream.
> Rising and rising behind the bars
> Of the convent, now the asylum, rose
> That woman's scream, a sound of beating, soon
>
> The roses shook in the sun as fists, and the sun
> Shook like a colossal Mandarin rose, and there ran
> Extraordinary grape shadows on the hot stone
> Walls. Then stillness.
>   Understand
>
> That was Vadstena: a scream, a beating, rising
> As a gigantic reeling stalk and the roses' fume
> Swelling all of a sudden, till their odour
> Colours, sickens, sounds.

1966

Good Vibes

(for Shena Mackay)

PETER PORTER

If you hadn't noticed the unprominent sign
We'd have missed Adlestrop, missed the gone
Railway and the bullock raking his back
In the hollow holly-bower. Missed, too, the sky
So intolerably lofty in its beakered blue
And the loping dog which frightened me
(Which is how I knew he was friendly) –
Most noticeably missed the station bench
And Adlestrop, the railway sign, with Edward
Thomas's poem on a plaque for pilgrims –
Not a great poem, but rich in names
And heartache and certainly a focus for
A sinisterly fine October afternoon.
Down one lane adjacent to the Home for Children
(With what impediment was never found)
All the day labourers of Oxfordshire and Gloucestershire
Were about their honey-making masonry
Of Cotswold stone, and the bullocks were nifty
In the meadow by the creek. There were no
Devils in the landscape, exhalations from
Ponds and dogs' breath and graveyards after rain
Could only be imagined in such unexpected sunshine,
But we felt them, felt a new humidity,
Oppressive like the self. This was a short walk
On two pilgrimages, a look-back out of Hades,
Such as the gods provide for laughter in their
Chronicles. Yet that sound, that risible division,
Strikes mortal earth some otherwise – such as
Gravel flicking from a low-slung bumper
A trailing jet above, a jostling on the eaves
Of sycamores. It was as if the well-intentioned
Dead were breathing out and blessing everyone,
Vibrations of the minute, without franchise,
A pointless benediction. Thinking again, I feel

Grateful that you saw through the uncleaned windows
A name which meant the same to all half-educated
Persons. To have trod on ground in happiness
Is to be shaken by the true immortals.

1975

Adlestrop: Among the Nation's Favourites

ANNE HARVEY

In 1948 when Roland Gant edited *The Prose of Edward Thomas*, he remembered being a schoolboy in an English lesson.

I can recall quite clearly my first contact with the work of Edward Thomas. It was ten or eleven years ago, sitting in a classroom one dull winter afternoon, flicking over the pages of a poetry anthology, feeling cold and bored. A poem entitled *Adlestrop* caught my eye:

> Yes. I remember Adlestrop—
> The name, because one afternoon
> Of heat the express-train drew up there
> Unwontedly. It was late June.

I read it through and the classroom with its droning voices and smell of dust, and the rain-drenched trees outside the window receded with the dismal winter day, and in my mind I saw the red of willow-herb by the river and heard the sound of bees in the warm June air. I had time to feel all this intensely before being jerked back to the present by the scratch of chalk on the blackboard.

I took the book home and read this and other poems, read the note about the poet who was killed at Arras before I was born. His poetry appealed to me because he seemed to say all the things I felt but was unable to say, and he said them so simply and with apparent ease. I was fortunate in having a good friend in the English master. He told me what he knew of Edward Thomas and I borrowed and bought those of his books I could find. When I walked in the country I carried a book of his poems or his *Songs and Poems for the Open Air*. So, gradually, over many years I read and re-read his poems, *The*

Heart of England, Rose Acre Papers, The South Country, and eventually all his other books. I discovered, too, those wonderful little books by Helen Thomas, *As It Was* and *World without End*, and read of their life together which must surely remain as one of the most beautiful and touching love-stories of our times. I began to feel that Edward Thomas was more than a man who had lived, written, and died. I felt that I knew him personally, that I had walked the lanes and the downs with him, had stopped at inns and talked with tramps and ploughmen at his side.

One evening, in a German prison-camp, I was talking about him to a group of Americans. One of them asked me whether I were related to Edward Thomas because I spoke of him so intimately and could obviously not have known him during his lifetime. It is true that for me, and for many others, his spirit is as living as the countryside of which he wrote.

Christopher Somerville similarly recalled: 'Like most of Edward Thomas's admirers I cut my teeth on "Adlestrop" . . . later I read my way from end to end of his work and had my own eyes and ears tuned to the subtleties of landscape and weather both on the ground and in the heart.'

In 1993 actress Jane Asher was one of many celebrities invited to choose a favourite poem for a collection called *I Remember, I Remember*. Choosing 'Adlestrop' she added: 'It is hard to say why this particular poem moves me so much – if I could put into words exactly what it means to me I'd be a poet myself! I've loved it since my schooldays.'

The appeal of the poem for children is intriguing. Kaye Webb, when editor of Puffin Books, edited an anthology, *I Like This Poem*, for the International Year of the Child, allowing children to make the choice. Fiona Cumberpatch said about 'Adlestrop': 'I find this poem peaceful and tranquil and when reading it I always feel soothed and calmed. I particularly like the final line as the thought of all those birds singing at once delights and fascinates me.'

Were those the reasons that prompted an eight-year-old Sheffield girl to send her mother up to her school with a problem: 'Her father says he'll take her anywhere she likes for her birthday . . . and well . . . she wants to go to Adlestrop and we don't know where it is.'

As an anthologist the anthology aspect interests me. So often one poem by a poet becomes his or her most popular, most quoted, most collected. 'Adlestrop' has joined such favourites as Kipling's 'If', Tennyson's 'Lady of Shalott', Walter de la Mare's 'The Listeners' and Masefield's 'Cargoes'.

One could blame editors for being like sheep: too lazy to pick the unusual, the off-beat, or even to read a poet's whole works – so much simpler to filch from another editor's findings. But it could be that 'the Nation's Favourites' have something special and indefinable to offer, something that captures the reader, something memorable.

'Adlestrop' was among the first poems written by Edward Thomas at the start of 1915 following that now well-documented summer of 1914 when the group known as the Dymock Poets gathered on the borders of Gloucestershire and Herefordshire, and Thomas and the American poet, Robert Frost 'pursued' – as Eleanor Farjeon noted in *The Last Four Years* – 'what seemed to be an endless duologue on the nature of poetry'. On walks, reminiscent of those taken by Coleridge and Wordsworth, these two talked of

> the 'cadence' in the human voice which accompanied the speech that came naturally to it, and Edward's own cadence was made clearer to himself so that those who ever heard the movement of his beautiful reflective voice can hear it now in the simplest utterance of a small unforgettable poem

> Yes. I remember Adlestrop—

The cadence is there, and out of the poet's lingering recollection a blackbird sings close by.

'Unforgettable' – perhaps that word provides the answer. On the last count 'Adlestrop' appears in thirty of the anthologies on my own book-shelves. My choice, though wide, is personal; my findings are informal. Thomas's poems filtered into anthologies after his death in 1917, but the first inclusion I can find is, appropriately, in *Come Hither*: a collection of rhymes and poems for the young of all ages made by his friend, Walter de la Mare, in 1923.

Ironically, in 1929, Harold Monro includes it in the Phoenix Library edition *Twentieth Century Poetry*; ironically because, back in 1915, Harold Monro, doyen of the Poetry Bookshop and *Poetry and Drama*, rejected Thomas's first poems. When Monro approached Helen Thomas, following her husband's death, about publishing the poems, she refused, reminding him, 'I remember well his hurt at your refusal.'

Monro's anthology introduction states:

> Many of the show poems of other anthologies have been omitted. Such are The Listeners, Cargoes, Innisfree, The Dead, Leisure, Music Comes, The Oxen, The Bells of Heaven, The Shepherdess . . . 'But' it may be asked . . . 'if these have been so loudly acclaimed, must they not be among the best poems of their respective authors?' I cannot answer. I only know that it has become so much a habit to reprint and to quote them, that for fear of making any of them an Excelsior or a Casabianca, it seemed necessary to exclude.

'Adlestrop' had not yet, then, reached that status.

Now it appears in a wide range of anthologies for readers of all ages; it is a poem that has crossed the child–adult barriers, has become a classic. In 'seasonal' collections it is a must under 'June' or 'Summer'. It serves editors well under 'Travel', even finding a space in Jennifer and Graham Curry's *Round the World in 80 Poems* (1988). Pamela Whitlock's fine *All Day Long* (1954) has a selection titled 'Railway Lines'. Robert Louis Stevenson's 'From a Railway Carriage' is there, of course, and I wonder if Edward Thomas knew this poem in childhood and remembered the meadows, horses, cattle, the painted stations whistling by, the mill, the river – 'each a glimpse and gone for ever'. Along with 'Adlestrop' Whitlock includes Eleanor Farjeon's 'The Child in the Train', where the young passenger watches:

> The buttercup embankments,
>   The telegraph wires,
> The names of the stations . . .

and a section of Aldous Huxley's 'Out of the Window' which reminds us

> In the middle of countries, far from hills and seas
> Are the little places one passes by in trains
> And never stops at . . .
> The glimpse of a sudden opened gate
> Piercing the adverse walls of fate . . .
> A moment only . . .

In *The Poetry of Railways* (1978) Samuel Carr observes: 'Poetry about trains . . . thanks to its subject is seldom uninteresting', although he does note 'Artists and Poets alike seemed often to have an imperfect understanding of the mechanics of railway travel'.

Peggy Poole, introducing *Marigolds Grow Wild on Platforms* (1996), writes:

In February 1995 I suddenly became obsessed with the idea of an anthology of railway poems, and immediately they began to fly at me from every direction in bewildering numbers. Why is it that trains and everything associated with them evoke such a massive response? Is it because our awareness is heightened when we travel, our antennae wave frantically, our emotions are hopelessly mixed, everything has a double or treble meaning? . . . There is, of course, time for reflection on a journey, reflection about the past and the future, about our place in the scheme of things. . . .

In 1943 G. Rostrevor Hamilton and John Arlott edited *Landmarks* and explained: 'Our general rule has been to confine ourselves to verse which is truly topographical, that is to say, which is strictly concerned with the spirit or appearance of a particular place or district.'

A setting of 'Adlestrop' by Gordon Jacob, 1958.

Johnny Coppin's *Forest and Vale and High Blue Hills* (1993) contains poems of 'Gloucestershire, the Cotswolds and Beyond'. A singer and musician, he tells readers:

> I so clearly remember my first vivid impression of the Cotswolds and Gloucestershire, as I travelled by train from Paddington to Cheltenham many years ago. As the train sped along the single track from Swindon, across the hills and down into the Stroud Valley, time appeared to stand still, and the villages and farms seemed to grow out of the landscape. . . .
>
> . . . Gradually I began to appreciate Gloucestershire and the Cotswolds more fully; to know its secret valleys, tiny churches, and the contrasts of its seasons, and also to understand its deep sense of history and how this has shaped the England of today. I soon began to realise how the landscape has been, and still is, such an inspiration to generations of musicians, artists, designers, craftsmen, and particularly poets and writers.

Antonia Fraser in her *Oxford and Oxfordshire in Verses* (1982) covers a smaller, but very rich, area, with an introduction that would have pleased Edward Thomas:

> . . . The poems I have chosen make up the images of my Oxford past, arranged alphabetically – by image, not author's name. In other words, here

are poems from Adlestrop to Zuleika. After all, does not Adlestrop generously embrace all the birds of Oxfordshire in its last line? . . . These, then, are the images which swirl about my head when I think of Oxford, settling like a kaleidoscope, now in one pattern, now in another. After completing the anthology I found that when I recited all the names together – aloud, as in the days of yore – I had created my own kind of Oxford and Oxfordshire rune, a sort of stream of past consciousness. Thus: 'Adlestrop, August, Addison's Walk, Academics, Bells, Birds . . .'

Margaret Drabble, following in the footsteps of the Literary Pilgrim in *A Writer's Britain* (1979), writes:

There are poems of Thomas's that seem to glimpse into the heart of England, to make, as R.S. Thomas has said, 'the glimpsed good place permanent'. One of his most famous poems, 'Adlestrop', catches the age and the place in four short stanzas. . . .

This is England, seen so briefly, so accidentally, so lastingly, from a passing train: who has not seen it so, and do we not all at times wonder if this is the only way to see it? There is no stopping: the train moves on.

'There is nothing new in the idea of an anthology about England' writes Richard Ingrams, editor of *England* (1989), later suggesting that:

while on the surface everything has changed, nothing has really changed at all. We still have our unique and unpredictable climate, believed by so many to be responsible for the national character; and in spite of what you read there is still a great deal of countryside left. . . . Perhaps the whole fun of any anthology such as this is to draw attention to these examples of consistency and to reassure ourselves that we remain much as we have always been. All that it amounts to is that the past can never be discounted. However many city centres are redeveloped, however many fields are built over it is with us whether we like it or not. And the best writing takes it always into account.

Sounds Good: Poems to be Heard (1998) is the most recent anthology containing 'Adlestrop' that has come my way, and editor Christopher Reid's introduction is pertinent:

The poems that get under one's skin in childhood, or at any early stage, should be treated with special respect. I have included a good many here from my own early reading, among them Masefield's 'Cargoes', Shakespeare's 'When icicles hang by the wall', Burns's 'To a Mouse', Edward Thomas's 'Adlestrop' and Keats's 'La Belle Dame sans Merci'. They are here, not for nostalgic reasons, but because the patterns a young mind could respond to in them turn out to speak with undiminished force to the mature reader capable of analysing their working parts. . . .

Edward Thomas himself edited some anthologies, among them *Poems and Songs for the Open Air* and *This England* and wrote in the magazine *Poetry and Drama* in 1914:

The anthologist should take either the best things or the representative things, or everything of a particular kind or of several kinds. . . . He should offer us what we lack skill or opportunity to find for ourselves, or he should make an arrangement of pieces in order to give us some special pleasure or to drive home some point.

PS: Not Only But Also . . .

A trend of the 1990s has been to invite readers, listeners and viewers to send, phone, fax or e-mail their favourite poems to the media. The winners are then published in the press or read by celebrities on radio or television programmes, or recorded for audio books. In this way their popularity is increased.

The *Independent* included 'Adlestrop' in its 'Daily Poem' slot during 1997. Literary editor Boyd Tonkin, confirming this, added:

I've always loved it though it's terribly hard to separate its haunting qualities as a poem from knowledge of Edward Thomas's fate. So I hear the names of regiments in Oxfordshire and Gloucestershire – does everyone else?

On 8 May 1998 it was Trevor McDonald's 'Anthology Choice' in the *Daily Telegraph*, one of several Thomas poems he has included.

On 2 January 1999 Andrew Motion, well known for his perceptive writing on Edward Thomas, chose Thomas's *Poems 1917* for his choice, no. 50, in the *Daily Telegraph*'s 'Book of The Century' series. The accompanying article begins:

Some books change the world by smashing into it like a meteor; others exert their influence quietly, working by slow degrees. Edward Thomas's first collection, *Poems (1917)* could hardly have begun life more modestly.

He describes Thomas's work as

a tough hinge between the Georgian world in which it was written and the contemporary world in which it has survived. It is full of time-honoured loyalties, and also of contemporary disruptions; it is wise about things which need to be preserved, and also responsive to change.

That short article prompted me to return to a much earlier piece that Motion wrote for *Poetry Wales* in 1978, in which he acknowledged Edward Thomas's

helping hand in my attempts to capture the inflections of a speaking voice . . .

as well as

the controversial cadence that Thomas captures in poems such as 'Adlestrop' and 'The Brook'.

Shortly after his appointment as Poet Laureate in May 1999 Andrew Motion chose not 'Adlestrop' but another much loved Thomas poem, 'Old Man', as his favourite poem on Radio 4's *Any Questions*.

Edward Thomas is frequently named 'the poet's poet'. At the dedication of the Memorial to First World War Poets in Westminster Abbey on 11 November 1985, the late Ted Hughes told Thomas's nephew, Edward Eastaway Thomas, 'He is the father of us all'.

The *Collected Poems* (1978 edition) was one of John Carey's '50 Books for the Millennium' in the *Sunday Times*. Expanding on his choices, Carey wrote:

Edward Thomas had a wholly distinctive poetic voice. All poets must sound like themselves, not like someone else if they are any good. But Thomas's voice is not only distinctive, it is also elusive, like a persistent regretful note heard at the edge of hearing. . . . His cadences stay with you for life, altering the way you feel. They are the sound of a mind communing with itself, resigned, scrupulously honest.

In 1997 listeners to Mike Read's Classic FM programme voted 'Adlestrop' number 23 of 'Your 100 Favourite Poems'. It appears in the book of that name and is read by Nicola McAuliffe on the audio recording.

'In 1995, to coincide with National Poetry Day, the BBC programme *The Bookworm* conducted a poll to discover the Nation's Favourite Poem' writes Griff Rhys Jones in the Foreword to the ensuing anthology. 'Adlestrop' came in at 20 here, just after Auden's 'Stop All the Clocks' and just before Brooke's 'The Soldier'. Griff Rhys Jones wrote to me:

It's a great poem. Like so many which anthologise well it seems to exactly capture a precise moment of experience which is both personal and universal at the same time.

Is it because the glimpse from a train of a station name in the heat is such a potent snapshot of lost opportunity? It is the quintessence of an ephemeral moment: so much promise framed in the window, so close but unobtainable. I don't know at all. I am suspicious of analysis these days. I love it, though.

Poetry Please, the Radio 4 programme, often invites listeners' requests and has featured 'Adlestrop' several times. In recent years Dannie Abse included it among his personal choices, as did actor Geoffrey Palmer, who told presenter Gareth Owen:

It's an exquisite poem. I had read it . . . I did know it . . . then fifteen years ago I was sadly at a memorial service and Judi Dench read it and I think it was one of the first times I realised how wonderful a poem is when read, as opposed to on the page . . .

[and, after reading the poem, he added]

Amazing, I think. . . .

Gareth Owen: It's the kind of moment that everyone's experienced in some way. Geoffrey Palmer: That's right. HE does it for all of us.

Radio 4's *Desert Island Discs* had no record of a single request for the poem, but in December 1974 critic and poet P.J. Kavanagh chose Edward Thomas's *Collected Poems* along with the Bible and Shakespeare's Works for his desert island reading.

The magazine *The Oldie* has a page where a well-known personality chooses six 'Pin-ups'. In February 1999 Stephanie Cole's four female choices were Margaret Rutherford, Mo Mowlam, Hildegard of Bingen and Dame Cicely Saunders. Her two males were the Dalai Lama and Edward Thomas . . . 'for writing some of my favourite poetry and prose and for penning the thought

Or shall I be content with discontent
As larks and swallows are, perhaps, with wings?'

She recalled how deeply 'Adlestrop' affected her at the time of the popular TV series *Tenko*, that most moving drama of women in a Japanese prisoner of war camp:

It was an episode in the second series . . . all the women were in a hut reminiscing about England and Stephanie Beacham's character, Rose, suddenly started to recite the poem . . . all the women went very quiet and the scene ended on the silence of remembering and the faces of Stephanie, Ann Bell and myself. It was the most potent way of encapsulating home and all it meant . . . far more than pages of dialogue could have done.

Jill Hyem, one of the script writers for the series, said that both she and Anne Valery, who wrote that particular episode, were keen on poetry and had read in the diaries that the women used to play games, remembering favourite poems, and sometimes had poetry recitals. She added:

> I had someone reading the 'These I have loved' sequence from Rupert Brooke's 'The Great Lover' in another episode. . . . 'Adlestrop' is a great favourite in our family. My mother used to recite it to us as children, then my son learnt it for one of those Guildhall exams and so it became part of the next generation's folk history. It is so English and uplifting.

> What will they do when I am gone? It is plain
> That they will do without me as the rain
> Can do without the flowers and the grass
> That profit by it and must perish without.
> I have but seen them in the loud street pass;
> And I was naught to them. . . .

Birtley Aris

wrote Edward Thomas in one of his poems. If he truly believed that, then the interest in his work today and the surprising attention paid to one particular poem would, one hopes, have pleased him.

Thomas would find that artists, too, have been inspired by his writing. 'Adlestrop' has been illustrated many times in books and magazines and has appeared on posters. In 1995 it was a *Poems on the Underground* choice, to be read on a London tube train at leisure or caught in rush-hour glimpses under someone's strap-hanging arm. It was also a striking Poets' Corner poster on the Dublin Railway, the DART, part of Jonathan Williams Poetry in Motion project. Much earlier, in the 1970s Birtley Aris's evocative interpretation of 'Adlestrop' was a MidNag publication, now a collector's treasure.

In January 1975 Radio 3 broadcast a play, also called *Adlestrop*, written by Roger Frith, who recalls:

Adlestrop was born out of an intense spiritual relationship with a Catholic married woman whom I'd met on a diesel train travelling between my home and London. I remember I wanted to take her to my childhood village in Leicestershire, if we could have gone there by steam train, but its little station had fallen under Beeching's axe. Adlestrop had always seemed to me (in the context of E.T's poem) to represent such stations, and when I came to write the play, it had to stand in for my own. But I chose it for another reason as well: I'd always felt, reading the poem, that someone did get off (E.T's ghost?). For my purposes, it was the woman's husband. . . .

The *Radio Times* billing reads: 'Roger Frith, the poet, meditates on the irreconcilability of spiritual and physical love.' . . . That's the play in a nutshell.

The two characters were played by Judi Dench and Edward Petherbridge. The play is compelling, having something of the mood of *Brief Encounter* while moving into a quite different territory.

Adlestrop

ROGER FRITH

Bird song for a Summer evening in Gloucestershire. Fully realistic.
SHE: (SOFTLY)   Darling: (PAUSE)   Darling.   (TO HERSELF) He's
   asleep.   (IN THE PAUSE AFTER THIS A BLACKBIRD IS HEARD FOR
   AN INSTANT DOMINATING THE OTHERS. SHE QUOTES MEDITATIVELY:
   HAS DIFFICULTY IN REMEMBERING THE WORDS) A blackbird song –
   close by, and round him, mistier – all the birds of Oxfordshire
   and Gloucestershire. (IN THE DISTANCE A DIESEL TRAIN CAN BE
   HEARD AND THIS IS HELD UNDER FOR ANNOUNCEMENT)

ANNOUNCER   Adlestrop by Roger Frith with Judi Dench and
   Edward Petherbridge.
   THE DIESEL TRAIN GATHERS FORCE, PEAKS AND PASSES MERGING INTO
   A STEAM TRAIN WHICH DEVELOPS INTO A MELODIC PATTERN. BLENDED
   WITH THIS PATTERN HER VOICE SWAYING TO IT, SHE CAN BE HEARD VERY
   QUIETLY AND SLIGHTLY DISTORTED.

SHE: Asleep – he's asleep.
   FADE STEAM AND BIRDSONG TO SILENCE

SCENE: A STATION. NOT RUSH HOUR. IN FACT, SILENT, BUT FOR THE HISSING OF A STEAM TRAIN. HOLLOW FOOTSTEPS. A CARRIAGE DOOR OPENING, CLOSING, THEN AFTER A PAUSE:

SHE: We just made it.

HE: Only just.

SHE: How dark the Down platform is.

HE: . . . We still haven't got any tickets.

SHE: We can get them from the ticket inspector.

HE: I've no money.

SHE: Neither have I . . . what did I do with my . . .

HE: (LAUGHING) British Rail will never pay with passengers like us.

SHE: Strange there was no one at the barrier.

HE: There often isn't.

SHE: Where are we anyway?

HE: I can't be certain.

SHE: I'll ask the ticket inspector.

HE: If there is one.

SHE: If, in your book, means hopeless.

HE: Not any more.

SHE: (AFTER A PAUSE) It's not a corridor train.

HE: We'll have to explain everything at the other end.

SHE: The point is not so much where we are, but where we are going to.

9.30 *Stereo*
Drama Now

Adlestrop by ROGER FRITH
with **Judi Dench**
and **Edward Petherbridge**
In this play for two voices,
Roger Frith, the poet, meditates on the irreconcilability
of spiritual and physical love.
' I believed I had a soul when
I didn't possess you. I had to
believe it. There would have
seemed no recompense for
having spent my life without
you otherwise.'
Special sounds by DICK MILLS of
the BBC Radiophonic workshop.
Technical assistants AMNA SMITH
and ANTHEA DAVIES
Producer HALLAM TENNYSON

HE: We're going to where I was evacuated during the War.

SHE: (AFTER A PAUSE) Why aren't there any announcements?

HE: Perhaps there's a strike.

SHE: If there's a strike, this train wouldn't be running.

HE: True. Ah, we're moving.

SHE: But where to?

HE: (LAUGHING) O dark, dark, dark, they all go into the dark . . .

SHE: What do you mean?

HE: It's just occurred to me we might be on the train to Eternity you once wished we <u>had</u> been on.

SHE: Don't joke. There's still Michael.

HE: Perhaps he'll be following on the milk train.

SHE: (AFTER A PAUSE) Strange, there seems to be no Up line.

HE: No what?

SHE: No line going back to the station. No opposite track.

HE: You can't see for the dark.

SHE: Dark. . . . And yet I don't see my reflection in the carriage window.

HE: I see you.

SHE: I see you too. . . . Another thing, we should be breathing heavily after that dash.

HE: But we're not. (STEAM TRAIN STARTS) Do you hear the engine?

SHE: Why?

HE: It's steam.

SHE: Steam?

HE: Yes, a steam engine. Not diesel.

SHE: What of it?

HE: 'The steam hissed. Someone cleared his throat.
        No one left and no one came
        On the bare platform. . . .'

SHE: What?

HE: 'Adlestrop'.

SHE: Adlestrop?

HE: That's where the train's going. That's where I was evacuated. Look at the old advertisements. I used to think some of them represented not Bognor or Bournemouth, but Paradise.

            . . . .

LATER, TOWARDS THE END OF THE PLAY . . .
                (FADE OUT . . . FADE UP)

HE: What happened next? I can't remember. Did we get off that train and part, or did it go on?

SHE: You know it went on.

HE: But were we on it?

SHE: We were on it, though we weren't . . .

HE: (AFTER A PAUSE) The lights have gone out!

SHE: But look, there's some light outside!

HE: Look at the sun there!

SHE: It's early morning.

HE: But where?

SHE: I know this countryside.

HE: So do I. It's like Oxfordshire.

SHE: I've been here with you!

HE: The train's slowing up.

SHE: It's a summer morning.

HE: But where?

SHE: I think it's Adlestrop!

Following the broadcast one listener, Dennis Briggs, wrote to the author:

> Dear Mr Frith . . . Apart for the first few moments I was fortunate to hear the whole of *Adlestrop* on Radio 3 last Wednesday. I found your theme and the way in which you developed the theme intriguing. But what I found compulsive and in a sense almost disturbing was your choice of journey viz – a steam train to Adlestrop, and the reasons given for this particular background. I was such an evacuee. I first set foot on Adlestrop station on the 1st September 1939 with my mother, having travelled straight from London.
>
> In fact I lived in the village of Adlestrop for several of the war years. The background you built for your play was so disconcertingly realistic for me that I feel bound to write to you in order to ask why you chose it. Was this in any way autobiographical? If so, did we ever meet, I wonder? If it is not so I am interested to know something of the reasons for your choice. . . .

There never had been a meeting. Many children, like Dennis Briggs, were evacuated to Adlestrop during the Second World War, and will have alighted at a fairly busy station, complete with welcoming nameboards on either platform.

As a postscript to Roger Frith's play, in *Lifelines*, an anthology edited by school students from Wesley College, Dublin, well-known people submitted favourite poems, with proceeds going to third world charities. Judi Dench chose 'Adlestrop'

> because of its essential Englishness and because it reminds me of the time of steam trains and that special hiss that announced their arrivals and departures.

Not Adlestrop

DANNIE ABSE

Not Adlestrop, no – besides, the name
hardly matters. Nor did I languish in June heat.
Simply, I stood, too early, on the empty platform,
and the wrong train came in slowly, surprised, stopped.
Directly facing me, from a window,
a very, *very* pretty girl leaned out.

　　　　When I, all instinct,
stared at her, she, all instinct, inclined her head away
as if she'd divined the much married life in me,
or as if she might spot, up platform,
some unlikely familiar.

For my part, under the clock, I continued
my scrutiny with unmitigated pleasure.
And she knew it, she certainly knew it, and would not
glance at me in the silence of not Adlestrop.

    Only when the train heaved noisily, only
when it jolted, when it slid away, only *then*,
daring and secure, she smiled back at my smile,
and I, daring and secure, waved back at her waving.
And so it was, all the way down the hurrying platform
as the train gathered atrocious speed
towards Oxfordshire or Gloucestershire.

1968

The Railway Connection

ANNE HARVEY

The curious and intense pleasure that is given to many people by the watching and the study of railway trains, their engines, and the detail of their organisation is both an art and a mystery. It is an art because the pleasure to be had is exactly proportionate to the informed enthusiasm one puts into it. It is a mystery because, try as one will, it is impossible to explain to others exactly in what the pleasure consists. The connection between the sight of a railway engine and the quite deep feeling of satisfaction is very real for multitudes of people but it eludes rational analysis. You can perhaps say what it is about railways you enjoy most but if somebody asks you why you should get any pleasure at all from what is no more than a handy method of conveying your person and your goods from one place to another, you can say, 'Just because it is so', and then you have nothing further to add to that bald and very unconvincing remark. The pleasure of railway watching cannot be explained, but it can perhaps be communicated and it can certainly be shared. . . . I have never met a lover of railways who felt the slightest need to produce any moral justification for his pleasure. Why should he? If he did, his pleasure would at once be heavily qualified. And I have met many, for we, the train lovers, are indeed a most numerous and varied company.

I begin to feel an affinity with Roger Lloyd, reading this piece from his book *The Fascination of Railways* (1951). Since researching 'Adlestrop' a new world has opened for me.

I am interested to know that Edward Thomas may have been on a train with four carriages – a third-class at each end with two composite middle carriages with one first- and one third-class compartment in each. Also that the engine <u>might</u> have been in the GWR City or Flowers 4–4–0 class (four small followed by four big wheels) and painted in the colour known as GWR Lake lined with yellow, which was introduced in 1912. There would have been a place for luggage, but no buffet carriage. Crisps, however, were in the shops by 1913.

I could almost sympathise with Bill Peto, Historical Research Officer of the Great Western Society Ltd, when he wrote to me: 'I was always extremely disappointed that Edward Thomas did not take the opportunity to note the name and number of the engine of the train.'

But Bill Peto, like all the railway enthusiasts I've met, knew all about 'Adlestrop'. He told me: 'When I was a young schoolboy in 1940 our English master introduced this poem which always appealed to me because it contained the name of a GWR station and I can still say without hesitation the first eight lines at least, even though it is fifty-nine years ago that I last heard of it.'

S.C. Jenkins and H.I. Quayle, writing of the Oxford, Worcester & Wolverhampton Railway in 1976, stress that it has always had a bad press and is one of the most slandered railways. I hasten to add that it was nothing to do with an unwonted stop at Adlestrop in June 1914 that gave it the name 'The Old Worse & Worse'! The OW & W has a long and fascinating history, and 'Adlestrop' has become part of it.

C.R. Potts, in *An Historical Survey of GWR Stations*, Volume IV (1985), supplies the following essential facts:

Origin: Oxford, Worcester & Wolverhampton Railway (became
            part of the West Midland Railway 1st July 1860;
            absorbed by GWR 1st August 1863)

Opened: 4th June 1853 (as 'Addlestrop & Stow Road',
            'Addlestrop' from 1st March 1862; altered to spelling
            shown in title from 1st July 1883)

Closed: 3rd January 1966 (Passengers)
            26th August 1963 (Goods)

Plan Date: 18th March 1910

At the opening, on 4 June 1853, the 40-mile portion of 'Cotswold Line' from Wolvercot Junction to Evesham was mixed gauge single track throughout, with a narrow gauge passing loop at Charlbury. A number of intermediate short loops

One of the cylinder 'Saint' class of locomotives, backing onto its train at No. 1 platform, Paddington, prior to departure. The coach livery here is in GWR Dark Lake of the 1914–16 period. Note the large 17 gallon milk churns to the right of the photograph. It used to be possible to roll two of these along on their bottom rims, one to each hand, but one had to be an expert! The fine, gleaming (if austere) locomotive was built in March 1913.
It is not possible to locate the exact train on which Edward Thomas travelled. One informed suggestion is that he 'could have been on a train pulled by one of the French "de Glehn" locomotives bought by GWR to compare new technical ideas'. (Photograph by Bill Kenning (aged thirteen), 19 December 1913)

were provided, but the line was worked as two sections, Wolvercot Junction to Charlbury and Charlbury to Evesham, until 18 November 1853, when the first 4 miles from Wolvercot Junction to Handborough became double track. The next 6 miles forward to Charlbury were doubled on 1 August 1854. However, the section between Charlbury and Campden, on which Adlestrop was located, remained single until 2 August 1858. Adlestrop was equipped with a broad gauge passing loop but as the only broad gauge train to use the line was the Inspection Special, two days before opening day, this was of no use whatsoever! (Readers puzzled as to why broad gauge rails should be provided and not used are referred to the entertaining chapter on the West Midland Railway in Edward MacDermot's *History of the Great Western Railway* (1973).

Oliver Lovell of the Cotswold Line Promotion Group, which safeguards and supports the Hereford–Worcester–Oxford Railway Line, reminded me that Dr

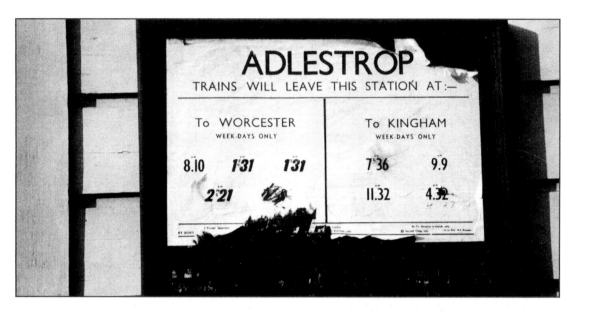

Richard Beeching's 1963 report – 'The Reshaping of British Railways' – lists the intended closure of every station on the line south of, but excluding, Kingham. Even Charlbury was on the list though this station was spared early on, and even retained its waiting-room fire after commuters petitioned against its replacement by an electric one. British Rail's chairman, Sir Peter Parker, was among the protesters.

There were disputes between passengers and staff at stations campaigning against the threatened closures; at one point the clerk to Kingham Parish Council went so far as to claim that Charlbury Station was nothing but 'a miserable, windswept little Halt' in comparison to Kingham. There was a major local campaign, headed by an indomitable Kingham lady, to save stations south of Kingham; and this sufficiently influenced the Minister of Transport to reprieve five Oxfordshire stations – Shipton, Ascott, Hanborough, Finstock and Combe – although all station buildings were demolished and train services and staff initially reduced.

'Had Adlestrop been south, rather than north of Kingham, or even in Oxfordshire rather than Gloucestershire, it might even be still open today. Food for thought!' says Mr Lovell.

Protestors, such as CLPG, made their mark. The line flourishes today with double the number of trains since the late seventies. But no trains stop at Adlestrop either intentionally or unwontedly. Worcester-bound trains stop at Kingham and 2 miles further on enter Gloucestershire, hurtling past the site of Adlestrop station where once the Evenlode flowed more pleasantly and there were well-cared for wooden station buildings, shiny advertisements and a trim garden.

The people of Adlestrop, however, did win the battle to save the station nameboard, or at least one of them.

Again and again books, magazines and newspapers repeat the story of the poem that made a station and a village famous. Quite apart from not getting the name of the train (or its number) Edward Thomas never alighted. Perhaps not many people know that he did have an early interest in railways, one that he wrote about very lovingly in his memoir *The Childhood of Edward Thomas* (1938), recalling holidays with his grandparents:

Swindon was a thousand time better. It was delicious to pass Wantage, Challow, Uffington, Shrivenham, to see the 75th, 76th mile marks by the railwayside, to slow down at last to the cry of 'Swindon' and see my grandmother, my uncle or my aunt waiting. My aunt was an attendant in the refreshment bar, and sometimes gave me a cake or sandwich to eat amid the smell of spirits, or took me to the private apartments, talking in a high bright voice and showing me round to various other neat women in black with high bright voices and nothing but smiles and laughs. My uncle was a fitter in the Great Western Railway works and knew everybody. He was tall, easy-going, and had a pipe in his mouth and very likely a dog at his heels. I was proud to be with him as he nodded to the one-legged signalman and the man with a white apron and a long hammer for tapping the wheels of all the carriages.

What he Heard

MONICA HOYER

He saw very little of Adlestrop . . .
only the name;
but the birds of two counties filled his ears,
on cue from Stationmaster Blackbird.

1993

The Train

CHLOE EDWARDS

'Pshhhhhhhhhhh', says the train,
As it glides from the station.

I stand in the corridor,
Leaning out of the window
Waving goodbye to a friend.

'Cli-cke-ty Clack' says the train,
As the engine wakes up.

The cool breeze tousles my hair
The smell of fresh cut grass
Floats past my nose.

'Clickety, Clickety, Clack.
Clack, Clack, Clickety'
Says the creaky old train.

The wind tickles my face.
I giggle.

'Giggly clack, giggly-clack,' echoes the train.

There is a woman in that field.
Whoooooooo? asks the train.

A fat white woman whom nobody loves?
Does she wear gloves? Giggle.

'Clickety clack, Clickety-Clack.
Click-ety -clack, Cli-cke-ty clack, Cli-cke-ty CLACK!'

Are we at Adlestrop yet?

The author was aged fifteen and a pupil at Bedales School in 1987 when her poem was one of the winning entries in an inter-schools competition.

Back to the Railway Carriage

JOHN BETJEMAN

I want you to imagine yourself in the waiting-room of a railway station on a wet evening. You know the sort of room: let me recall it – a wind whistling down the platform, a walk battling against the breeze to the door marked General Waiting Room, the vast interior, the black horse-hair benches and chairs, the mahogany table, the grate with its winking fire, the large frame of yellowing photographs of crowded esplanades and ivy-mantled ruins, the framed advertisement for the company's hotel at Strathmacgregor – electric light, exquisite cuisine, lift to all floors, within five minutes of sea and pier – the gaslight roaring a friendly bass to restless conversation of other people also awaiting trains.

Just such a scene as this, which may be witnessed any evening at a hundred junctions, lost among the suburbs of industrial towns or far away in the country where branch line meets main line – just such a scene as this was witnessed sixty, seventy, eighty years ago. I shall have the railways complaining that I am calling them Victorian. Let them complain: They *are* Victorian, that is their beauty. But they are not only Victorian, they are Edwardian and modern as well.

Think yourself back into that waiting-room and learn with me the first lesson the railway teaches us – to pay a proper respect to the past. Railways were built to last. None of your discarding last year's model and buying this year's. That horse-hair seat has supported the Victorian bustle, the frock coat of the merchant going city-wards first-class, your father in his best sailor suit when he was being taken to the seaside, and now it is supporting you; and it's far from worn out. That platform has seen the last farewells of sons and parents, has watched the city man returning home to break the news to his wife that he's bankrupt, has watched his neighbour come in a new suit one morning and with a first-class, instead of a third-class, ticket. Turn from the human history to the history of stone and steam and iron. The railway station in the old days was a monument to science. Euston, whose fine Doric portico – one of London's noblest buildings – was the new gateway to the North; King's Cross whose simple outlines are a foretaste of all that is good in modern architecture; Temple Meads, Bristol, in the Tudor style, far from gimcrack, but cut out of local stone; Newcastle Central station, a lovely classical building, and many a lesser station. I know little stations among the Shropshire hills built in a solid but picturesque Gothic style to tone in with the romantic scenery. I know of huge suburban stations which are dusty from disuse and full of top-hatted ghosts in the corners of echoing gas-lit booking halls. Best of all I know that station in Cornwall I loved as a boy, the oil lights, the smell of seaweed floating up the estuary, the rain-washed platform and the sparkling granite, and the hedges along

the valleys around, soon to be heavy with blackberries. I think of Edward Thomas'
lovely poem on Adlestrop, a station in the Cotswolds.

> Yes. I remember Adlestrop–
> The name, because one afternoon
> Of heat the express-train drew up there
> Unwontedly. It was late June.
>
> The steam hissed. Someone cleared his throat.
> No one left and no one came
> On the bare platform. What I saw
> Was Adlestrop—only the name.

That verse recalls one of the deeper pleasures of a country railway station – its silence
broken only by the crunching of a porter's feet on the gravel, the soft country accent
of the station-master, and the crash-bang of a milk-can somewhere at the back of the
platform. The train, once in the centre of a noisy town, has drifted into the deep heart
of English country, with country noises brushing the surface of a deeper silence.
Edward Thomas expressed this in the last stanza of his poem on Adlestrop station:

> And for that minute a blackbird sang
> Close by, and round him, mistier,
> Farther and farther, all the birds
> Of Oxfordshire and Gloucestershire.

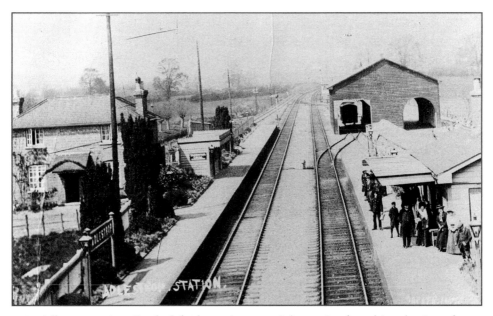

Adlestrop station. On the left, the stationmaster's house, 'up for sale' at the time of
researching this book.

You need never be bored in a train. You can always read a book, and an even more interesting book to read than that on your knee is the faces and habits of your fellow passengers. I know the types so well: the fussy type – the old person who wraps a travelling rug round his knees and gets up to lean out of the window at every station and ask if this is the right train for Evercreech, receiving the answer 'yes' every time. He continues to look out, as though his anxious face will cause the guard to blow his whistle sooner. The vacant fool who taps with his toes on the floor and whistles to hide his embarrassment when the train comes to an unexpected halt between stations. The talkative person who tries to get into conversation – the war has brought on a big increase in this type. You know the sort of thing. I enjoy seeing how long I can answer 'yes' and 'oh' without getting involved in conversation.

'Colder today, isn't it?'
'Yes'.
'But the days'll be getting longer soon.'
'Yes'.
'Does this train stop at Chippenham?'
'Yes'.
'Stops on the way first, I suppose?'
'Yes'.
'Got a married sister at Chippenham'.
'Oh'.
'But my Mother's family comes from Wootton Bassett'.
'Oh'.
'Come from Stoke Newington myself'.
'Oh'.

Then there's the lady who gets in with a friend. She gossips the whole way upon the advantages, or the disadvantages, of permanent waving, on whether to go back on the 5.18 or the 6.24, on the other hand if she catches the 6.24 she'll miss the 8.50 bus to Pinehurst turn and have to wait for the 9.40 unless the 8.50 hasn't gone or the train comes in earlier than schedule. But if she catches the 5.18, then there may not be time to get the stuff for the curtains, and then there's the wait for the 7.34 bus the other end, so it's hardly worth it really.

The only type of passenger whom I find it rather hard to stomach is the man who pares his nails with a penknife.

But the greatest gift the railways give to us is the proper treatment of time. Of course there are expresses that will hurtle you from place to place in no time. And there used to be cars volleying along a tarmac road at sixty miles an hour. But I prefer a leisurely journey in a stopping train, seeing the country, getting to the place much sooner and much more comfortably in the long run. And if the train is a bit late, what matter? There are one's fellow-passengers to study, the unfamiliar view of a place one knows well from the road seen at an odd angle from the railway, the photographs below the rack to look at, the railway noises to listen to. And for me there's the pleasure of a railway time-table. It's one of the ironies of this war that the centenary of Bradshaw, which occurred last November, should have been obscured by the war. The original Bradshaw was a Quaker and a great worker for peace. How I enjoy his pages – particularly those at the end which deal with the Great Southern Railway in Eire! 'Stops to take up at Inny Junction Halt on Thursdays and Saturdays'. Inny Junction Halt is hidden away among the footnotes of Bradshaw. What romance there is in the name! For Inny Junction is a station lost in an Irish bog in the middle of Westmeath: there's no road to it, nothing but miles of meadowsweet and bog myrtle and here and there the green patch and white speck of a distant Irish smallholding, and the silence is livened only by rumblings of distant turf carts and the hiss of a waiting Great Southern engine on Thursdays and Saturdays.

Trains were made for meditation. And I advise slow trains on branch lines, half empty trains that go through meadows in the evening and stop at each once oil-lit halt. Time and war slip away and you are lost in the heart of England.

BBC BROADCAST, 1940–5

Single to Adlestrop

MONICA HOYER

No, not safe-sounding Applethorpe,
but sudden Adlestrop,
as glimpsed by a passing poet
whose unforeseen stop
at the mongrel-named, deserted station,
was decades ago, when somebody coughed.

His lines preserve a strangeness . . .
the midsummer silence, and the name:
born of a misprint? —
a parish clerk to blame? —
and prick my nomadic inclination,
drawing it out to Adlestrop.

And the pull will ensure my presence —
by rickety branch-line . . . shanks' pony . . .
come Thomas's late June,
listening on the maverick-lonely
platform for his blackbird's exaltation
of oddness, and England,
where somebody coughed.

1993

'The Bare Platform'
(A Glimpse of Adlestrop in the 1930s)

CHRIS TURNER

When an express carrying the poet Edward Thomas came to rest at Adlestrop one afternoon in late June of 1914 the stillness there was sufficiently striking to inspire his famous lines.

Although hardly the busiest time of day, traffic at Adlestrop was nevertheless meagre. In the 1930s the number of tickets issued each year barely exceeded 2,000, from a peak of nearly 6,000 in 1903 (an average of about 20 per day), and many of the 40–50 season tickets were scholars' seasons issued to pupils travelling to Campden Grammar School. In 1938 only 1,424 tickets were issued (4 or 5 per day).

Parcels and miscellaneous traffic had also been in decline from a peak of just over 12,000 in 1913 to barely 2,000. Goods traffic had never been heavy, the total tonnage having dropped from 4,146 in 1903 to 1,406 in 1938. For most of the 1930s it had barely exceeded 2,000. Just over 100 wagons of livestock were being dealt with annually in the mid-1930s but only 31 wagons were handled in 1938.

According to official records, in 1925 Adlestrop was staffed by a station master, a Grade 2 porter, a junior porter and a signalman. In the late 1920s the signalman was replaced by a porter-signalman and the junior's post withdrawn, the work being covered by a junior based at Kingham. Further economies followed in the early 1930s when the Grade 2 porter was also withdrawn.

In the mid-1930s the station master was Bill Harris, who lived with his family in the station house. When Archie Warren first started working at the station in April 1935 as a junior porter based at Kingham, the station master covered the early turn and overlapped with the porter/signalman Tom Carey (later Harold Hall) who was on a permanent late shift.

Sadly, Bill Harris had to take early retirement due to failing eyesight, and after a brief period of cover by a relief station master, Fred Warren was transferred from Bloxham and promoted to Grade 1 porter to cover the post. From September 1938 the station came under the supervision of Mr Jones, the station master at Kingham, who visited the station twice a week, cycling out during the middle of the morning and returning at 11.44 on the 8.23 a.m. Wolverhampton to Paddington. It was at about this time that Fred Warren and Harold Hall alternated on early and late shifts.

Daily Routine

Covering the station master's post, Fred Warren worked from 7.0 a.m. to 4.0 p.m. with an hour's break for lunch. At this time he was living at Bledington with his parents and used a motorbike to get to work, and subsequently an Austin Seven which he parked opposite the station buildings. The only way onto the up platform was via a small gate at the south (Kingham) end of the station building, the keys to which were very unofficially kept inside the case of the oil lamp above the main doors. In the winter the lights were turned up and fires laid in the office and booking hall – 'I can't remember the fire in the Ladies ever being lit'.

Fred then remained in the office ready to book passengers for the first train, the 6.40 a.m. Worcester Shrub Hill to Paddington due just after 7.35. He also dealt with any outstanding paperwork and checked parcels which were awaiting collection or delivery. The DSO cash bag, prepared the previous day, was retrieved from the safe and put on the 7.32 a.m. Oxford to Worcester Shrub Hill, on which the junior porter, Archie Warren arrived at 8.25.

He had joined the GWR in April 1935 when he was fifteen years of age and became a junior porter at Kingham. His daily routine was shared between Kingham and Adlestrop.

Archie lived at Bledington with his parents and brothers and sisters, and cycled to Kingham where he booked on at 7.0 a.m., attending trains and dealing with cleaning duties there before travelling out to Adlestrop. The train always conveyed newspapers and periodicals as well as parcels, and on arrival Archie assisted with the unloading. The arrival of the train was anxiously awaited by Mr Hunt, the local newsagent, the newspapers and parcels being taken across the line by hand or barrowed, for him to start to sort out under the station canopy. Several members of staff from large houses like Adlestrop House and Daylesford House waited to collect their papers and when they'd been handed out, Hunt took the remainder to a nearby small wooden hut where he prepared for the various delivery rounds in the area.

Archie's duties included general cleaning of the station and the pumping of water into the toilet cisterns. Water appears to have been pumped up from below ground, possibly from a culvert which ran under the station at this point. He also dealt with the delivery of parcels after assisting the station master with the delivery sheet. He would often set off on foot with only a single parcel under his arm, but sometimes a two-wheeled barrow had to be used. 'I can only remember going to Oddington Post Office which was run by Mr and Mrs Peters.' Most parcels traffic was collected from the station. Fred Warren sometimes used his own car to deliver parcels.

Porter signalman Harold Hall arrived on the 8.23 a.m. Wolverhampton to Paddington, due at 11.43 and, if necessary, on arrival assisted the station master with the unloading of parcels. He then assisted with general station duties and delivery work, particularly on Mondays and Tuesdays when the junior porter was lamping. However, both he and the station master made sure they were in the office together ready for news of the arrival of the daily pick-up goods. The signalman at Kingham would ring to confirm if the train needed to call and Harold opened the signal box. 'If the goods was due to call on the return, I remained in the box until all the shunting was complete.' Harold had been promoted from Chipping Campden in about 1936.

'I had about a week with a district reliefman at Adlestrop but had to learn a lot myself.' He actually learned much of the work through the GWR correspondence courses as well as gaining experience of general railway work at other stations.

Harold recalls the rest of the shift as 'very quiet' and, after the station master left at 4.0 p.m., he spent most of the time in the office attending to any passenger and parcels traffic. He closed the station shortly after the departure of the 6.47 Worcester Shrub Hill to Oxford which left at 8.15 and then made his way over to the down platform to join the last train, the 7.42 Oxford to Shrub Hill diesel railcar due away at 8.29. 'I cannot remember any passengers joining or leaving this train.'

Incidentally, the porter/signalman was also required to open the signal box when a train had to be refuged.

Passenger Trains/Passengers

Down Service
Adlestrop was served by five trains, the first, the 7.32 a.m. Oxford to Worcester Shrub Hill, was used by several schoolchildren attending Campden Grammar School including the sons of Woolliams, the farmers. The only other regular for this train was a Miss Keen who worked at Moreton-in-Marsh. The remaining services, the 11.32 a.m. and 3.42 p.m. Oxford to Wolverhampton, the 4.45 Paddington and 7.42 Oxford (diesel car) both to Shrub Hill, were very poorly patronised.

Up Service
The first of the five services in the up direction, the 6.40 a.m. Worcester Shrub Hill to Paddington, arrived just after 7.35, then there was a long gap until the 8.23 Wolverhampton to Paddington at 11.43. The next, the 3.15 p.m. Worcester Foregate Street to Oxford (4.36), brought the grammar school children back, and just over an hour later the 4.55 p.m. Stratford-on-Avon to Oxford brought back Miss Keen. The last up train was the 6.47 Shrub Hill to Oxford which was due away at 8.15 p.m.

Working of Horse-Boxes and Cattle Wagons

When horse-boxes occasionally arrived on the rear of scheduled up passenger services, the train was set back from the platform to place the vehicles in the loading bank, adjacent to the goods shed. Similarly, loaded vehicles were also collected by passenger trains setting back to the bank. Horse-boxes for the opposite direction were collected by down trains which had to back into the yard from the Moreton end.

Wagons of sheep, and very occasionally cattle, arrived on goods trains which called specially. Invariably they arrived outside the station opening times and the staff had to be booked out on special duties. Fred recalled that once, by prior arrangement, he came on duty in the early hours of the morning to deal with a goods train which detached a wagon of sheep, which he thinks came from Scotland.

Farmer Woolliams of Evenlode came out specially to collect the sheep and drove them out along the road. Harold Hall also remembers opening the box to detach vehicles off the front of up and down passenger trains for a similar situation. 'After doing the work, I spent the morning walking around Adlestrop Park and returned late morning to begin my booked shift.'

Working of Goods Trains

Down Service

Adlestrop was served when required by the 8.30 a.m. Oxford to Moreton-in-Marsh pick-up goods which was scheduled to call from 1.54 to 2.32 p.m. This train, and its return, was usually worked by an Oxford crew and Jack Hewlett is remembered as one of the regular guards. As already explained, the signal box was opened for the working of both goods trains.

On arrival, the train either stopped on the down main, short of the crossover leading to the yard, or, when necessary, drew forward and set back into the down refuge siding. In either case, the guard secured the train and uncoupled the wagons for Adlestrop which were drawn forward and set back into the yard. The front portion of the train usually conveyed two station trucks, one from Bristol to Honeybourne and another en route from Didcot to Hockley. These were normally both 'on the engine' where they would remain during the shunting. The outwards wagons were usually collected and attached to the train before the inwards wagons were positioned. Any wagons which had to be sorted were stood aside and secured on the main line as necessary before being returned to the yard. Although Fred and Harold don't recall dealing with the station trucks. Archie certainly went to the goods shed to deal with 'smalls' traffic which presumably was unloaded there during a pause in shunting.

Up Service

The return working left Moreton-in-Marsh for Oxford at 2.50 p.m. and was booked to call at Adlestrop from 3.3 to 3.15, but Fred Warren could not remember the train calling and believes 'up line' traffic was taken through to Moreton by the down train. When the train did call to collect wagons, they had invariably already been positioned by the down train or pinch-barred from the loading dock by the station staff.

On a general point, empty wagons ordered away were usually formed together wherever possible so that on arrival at Moreton or Oxford they were shunted off in one cut to save time, particularly at Moreton where the main line often had to be occupied during shunting.

Harold Hall recalled that exceptionally, and dependent on its length, the up train was set back into the goods yard and through the shed to allow another train to pass.

Passenger Rated Traffic

General Parcels

Regular consignments included mail order catalogues and goods from Great Universal Stores and J.D. Williams, both of Manchester, and Kays of Worcester.

The presence of several large houses in the area gave rise to various types of traffic. Brigadier-General McCalmont of Adlestrop House spent regular periods in London and had a hamper of locally grown fruit and vegetables sent to him, the hamper being brought to the station by his staff. When his staff accompanied him on annual holidays, their luggage was sent in advance. Mrs Samuda of Oddington Lodge, Lower Oddington, sent a hamper of laundry each week to Shipton for a Mrs Miles of Milton under Wychwood. The hamper usually went up on the 8.23 a.m. Wolverhampton to Paddington and was apparently returned during a subsequent afternoon/evening.

Newspapers and Periodicals

Mr Hunt from the Oddington area received bundles of papers each morning on the 7.32 a.m. Oxford to Worcester Shrub Hill. Hunt was sometimes assisted by his son Bob, also apparently Miss Newman whose father was one of the Adlestrop platelayers.

As already stated, Hunt kept his supplies in a hut at the back of the up platform (behind the Gents) where he sorted them ready for delivery. Hunt had 'a two-wheeled cart with two handles so it could be pulled and pushed'. He used this to deliver daily newspapers to Adlestrop and Oddington and once a week even went as far as Bledington with periodicals. As a child in the 1920s, Fred Warren remembered Hunt using an old pram and delivering his copy of *The Rainbow*.

Perishables

Lyon's cakes were delivered regularly to Mr and Mrs Peters at the Post Office in Lower Oddington.

Twice a week a carton of pies arrived from Collins of Evesham. They were collected by Harry Jackson of Upper Oddington who delivered greengrocery locally.

Day-old chicks

Local farms occasionally received chicks, and Fred recalled one occasion when they arrived late and he delivered them using his car on the way home.

Horses

Percy Bolter, a horse dealer from Upper Oddington, sent away horses and occasionally ponies. The traffic was dealt with at the loading bank and the arrangements are discussed separately.

Cattle and sheep

Farming brothers Ernie Woolliams of Adlestrop and Robert of Evenlode received animals which were unloaded through the cattle pens. The most regular arrivals were sheep for Robert of Evenlode Grange. These were sent from Ashford, Kent, the Craven Arms area and apparently Scotland. They were driven out of the pens and along the road to the farm.

Goods Traffic

Coal

The only merchant remembered was a G.R. Williams who received supplies for Pratt & Haynes (Shipton) Ltd. Williams, who lived at Lower Oddington, had a wharf at the far end of the yard, beyond the goods shed and an office in the goods yard next to the weighbridge. He was assisted by his son and a Mr Gardner, and delivered supplies using a lorry. Harold Hall says Williams received 'only one or two trucks a week'.

Timber

Locally cut timber was brought up to the station by Messrs Claridge of Heythrop and stacked along the loading bank in the goods yard. Fred recalls 'it was the general rule for the railway to wait eight days before loading', the work being carried out by timber loaders from Worcester. They usually ordered two Macaw bogie bolster wagons which were loaded using a rail-mounted crane marshalled between them. The signal box was opened when loading was taking place because the crane jib fouled the up main line. The loaders arrived on the first up train, the 6.40 a.m. from Shrub Hill and returned shortly after 4.30 on the 3.42 Oxford to Wolverhampton. When the wagons had been loaded, they were usually collected by the down goods train, and if the work had been completed, the crane was also returned.

Tarmac (tarred chippings)

Fred remembered several sheeted open wagons of tarmac arriving (he believes from Coleford) for resurfacing Adlestrop Hill, leading to the Cross Hands public house. Cartage contractors unloaded the contents and took it to the site of work. 'This was the first time I had seen tarmac by rail and, as far as I was concerned, the first occasion I had seen it applied directly to a road surface.'

Hay

Wagon loads of hay were sent away by Mr Newton of Hook Norton, whose men collected it from local farms. Whe the wagons were loaded, the railway staff sheeted it. Harold Hall recalled that Newton insisted on three sheets, one in the centre and the others overlapping at each end.

Straw
Wagon loads were also occasionally despatched by Frost of Banbury and dealt with
in a similar way to the hay.

Building supplies
General material including bags of cement, sections of fencing, etc. arrived on the
station truck which was unloaded in the goods shed. Supplies for Howse, a builder
in the Stow Road, were collected by Harry Davis.

This article is reproduced from Great Western Railway Journal *No. 24,
Autumn 1997, by kind permission of Wild Swan Publications Ltd*

Adlestrop Revisited

(for Edward Thomas)

WILLIAM COOKE

Adlestrop ¾. A short drive off the hot road
through empty, narrowing lanes, the cows
somnolent, hay raising the barns' roofs,
horses tailing away late summer flies. Then,
at a fork, a bus-shelter shelters beneath
an oak, and inside the station nameboard hangs,
archaic in its cream and brown. Your poem's
there, a small plate on a solid platform bench,
for anyone to read who spends an idle moment
waiting for the bus. But principally for those
like me, who come to see a spot you only glimpsed
on that June afternoon before you went to war.

The way to the station's barred. Squeeze through
and find the station gone, the 'bare platform'
(or what's left) anonymous, derelict. Weeds
sprawl; a drift of logs sawn years before
smoulders to decay; an ancient bike corrodes.
Away from the bridge the silence is complete.
Sixty years on, no trains stop, no one notices
the place. And no more singing for the bird.

1978

Jane Austen and Adlestrop

ANNE HARVEY

Most articles and accounts of Adlestrop list Jane Austen and Edward Thomas under '*literary interest*', often just as a reference to her family and his poem. As neither actually lived there, they don't warrant an entry in most topographical books, but while Edward Thomas never even got off the train that stopped there, Jane Austen did visit the Adlestrop Leighs, her mother's family, at least three times. This association has not been overlooked, and there have been many attempts by biographers and researchers to identify actual places with those that appear in Austen's novels; certainly the claims made to link Adlestrop to *Mansfield Park* seem justified.

Adlestrop was one of the many estates inherited by Rowland Leigh, eldest son of Thomas Leigh of Stoneleigh, in the late sixteenth century. The Leighs chose to live at Longborough until the mid-seventeenth century when William Leigh made Adlestrop his home.

Mrs Leigh's second cousin, James Henry Leigh, was nominal head of the family, while her first cousin, the Revd Thomas Leigh, was Rector of Adlestrop. He and his

Adlestrop Park (1829), the manor house where Jane Austen's second cousin, James Henry Leigh, resided.

unmarried sister, Elizabeth, were godparents to Jane's sister Cassandra and brother Henry, and Jane herself was always made welcome. We know, from correspondence, that Jane and Cassandra visited Adlestrop in July 1794 when Jane was nineteen and again in 1799 when the Parsonage, or Rectory, had become known as Adlestrop House. They will have walked in the grounds and gardens of both this house and the Manor House, known as Adlestrop Park, and attended services presided over by Thomas Leigh, at the Church of St Mary Magdalene.

The most significant visit made by Jane Austen, accompanied by her mother and sister, was in the summer of 1806. Prior to this the Revd Thomas Leigh had taken it on himself to make substantial alterations to Adlestrop. These included the enclosure of the village green and the building of cottages to house those who had once lived in full view of the great house. Humphry Repton, the celebrated Homes and Gardens improver of

Jane Austen. (A watercolour by Cassandra Austen, 1804)

his day, visited Adlestrop to cast his expert eye over the work undertaken, and in his *Observations on the Theory and Practice of Landscape Gardening* (1803) he praises Leigh's work. This is not surprising as the rector will, no doubt, have been highly influenced by Repton.

One can imagine Jane listening to talk of Repton and comments on new fashions in design and landscape gardening, and then weaving them into her writing of *Mansfield Park*. The first hint of interest occurs with actual mention of Repton himself. We read that 'His terms are five guineas a day.' That voluble character Mrs Norris then recommended change at any cost, remembering how before her husband's death, 'We did a vast deal in that way at the parsonage; we made it quite a different place, from what it was when we first had it.' Discussion on improving one's property oneself, or engaging a professional, leads to Mary Crawford's statement: 'Had I a place of my own in the country, I should be most thankful to any Mr Repton who would undertake it and give me as much beauty as he could for my money; and I should never look at it, till it was complete.'

Adlestrop Rectory.

The Adlestrop changes coincide with Henry Crawford's idea for Edmund Bertram's Thornton Lacey Parsonage in *Mansfield Park*. Crawford's discovery of the village and parsonage in the novel might well describe Adlestrop:

I have never told you what happened to me yesterday in my ride home. . . . I told you I lost my way after passing that old farm house, with the yew trees, because I can never bear to ask; but I have not told you that with my usual luck – for I never do wrong without gaining by it – I found myself in due time in the very place which I had curiosity to see. I was suddenly, upon turning the corner of a steepish downy field, in the midst of a retired little village between gently rising hills; a small stream before me to be forded, a church standing on a sort of knoll to my right – which church was strikingly large and handsome for the place, and not a gentleman's house to be seen excepting one – to be presumed the Parsonage, within a stone's throw of the said knoll and church. I found myself in short in Thornton Lacey.

Crawford then proceeds to list the radical changes he has in mind which include turning the house to front the east instead of the north and making a completely new garden to give it 'the best aspect in the world'. Edmund Bertram's replies show that, probably like Jane herself, he 'must be satisfied with rather less ornament and beauty'.

There is too much emphasis on the subject of design and renovation to dismiss the coincidence; Jane Austen describes architecture and alteration with more than expected precision.

The Austens' 1806 visit occurred just after the death of the Honourable Mary Leigh, the wealthiest Leigh relative, at Stoneleigh Abbey in Warwickshire. Thomas Leigh had no sooner arrived home after the funeral, than his lawyer advised him to return to the Abbey to attend to business matters. Although some Austen research has implied that he left Adlestrop overhurriedly to ensure possession of the property, he was, in fact, only carrying out his duties as the lawful heir. An entourage accompanied his return to Stoneleigh; they included his sister, Elizabeth; his lawyer, Joseph Hill; and Mrs Hill; and his three Austen relatives.

Stoneleigh Abbey is recreated as Sotherton Court in *Mansfield Park*, a novel that the Revd Thomas Leigh is unlikely to have read as he disapproved of women engaging in such folly as writing. His own wife, Mary, had been encouraged by the former Indian pro-consul Warren Hastings (who, incidentally helped the Leighs in their planning and planting the Adlestrop trees) to borrow books from the library on his family estate at nearby Daylesford. Mary then took to writing herself. On Mary's death, Thomas Leigh blamed her ill-health on this activity, although it was far more likely because of the trauma caused by the deaths of numerous children in childbirth or infancy.

Edward Thomas, while not disapproving of women writers, only included one in his *A Literary Pilgrim in England* (a chore which he jokingly named 'OMES & 'AUNTS) and it was not Jane Austen; nor have I found a mention of her elsewhere in his writing. They did, however, both reside, at different times, in Hampshire, and the following facts intrigue me.

> *Mansfield Park*, with its Adlestrop references, was published in 1814.
> Edward Thomas's train stopped at Adlestrop in 1914.
> Jane Austen died in 1817.
> Edward Thomas died in 1917.

And in a small book of essays, *Personalia*, published in 1917, his writer and solicitor friend, E.S.P. Haynes wrote:

> In December 1898 Professor Morgan, a friend of and contemporary of mine at Balliol, brought an interesting compatriot of his to my rooms from Lincoln. Edward Thomas was then, as always, tall and thin. He had what another friend has described as a 'golden brown face' and deep blue eyes which sometimes became suddenly translucent and alert with interest. His voice was a singularly melodious tenor. He sang and read aloud very well. I have never heard so delightful a rendering of Jane Austen's novels or Gibbon's chapters on Christianity as he once gave me when I was ill. . . .

Adlestrop

(*To the memory of Edward Thomas*)

HARDIMAN SCOTT

Yes. I remember Adlestrop,
For I, too, was at Adlestrop
The other day – one afternoon
Early in July; not to stop

More than an hour or two, but long
Enough, it seemed, to meet with you
In and out of Time. There the station
Where your train had stopped, and a few

Young shorthorns grazing by the line,
The sunlight rusty on their flanks,
And willows; hay was done of course,
But meadowsweet was there, and banks

Meadowsweet (Latin *Ulmaria*)
or Queen of the Meadows.

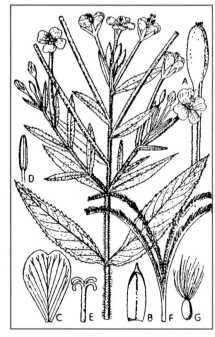

Great Willowherb, Codlins-and-cream,
Equilobrium hirsutum.

Of willow-herb like pink feathers
In the grass, and a blackbird – two
In fact, came chinking across the road
And vanished where brambles overgrew.

I found where the road twisted sharp
Into the village of Cotswold
Homes, and went into the little
Cottage post-office to be told

My way, but no-one was there. I'd
Come to see a farmer who'd been
Five years under these hills, but all
Was still in Adlestrop, and green

The tilting fields, and quiet too.
So that I wondered if your stop
And mine could have added meaning to
The singing birds in Adlestrop.

1972

Adlestrop: The Cottages and their Inmates

ANNE HARVEY

Rose Evelyn Cholmondeley.

No book about Adlestrop would be complete without reference to the Cholmondeley family who became prominent after the Leighs had departed for Stoneleigh in 1806.

The Hon. Revd (later Canon) Henry Pitt Cholmondeley married a sister of Lord Leigh of Adlestrop Park and was Rector of Adlestrop from 1852 to 1905. His fifty-three years in office are marked by the tallest cross in the churchyard of St Mary Magdalene, Adlestrop. He had eight children and his oldest son, Francis, succeeded him as Rector from 1905 to 1936. The marriage register shows that his oldest daughter, Mary Louisa, married Charles Mordaunt, Baronet of Walton Hall, released by divorce from his previous marriage. This information was provided by John Gillett, a resident of Adlestrop who has carried out some local research. He wonders, as I do, how the Rector justified this in 1878 . . . let alone how he hid the fact that one of his sons (Edmund? Harry? Charles?) fathered a child by one of the village girls working at the Rectory!

Eleanor Cholmondeley, known as Nellie was born in 1857 at the Rectory and grew up to be a most formidable lady, ruling her father, then her brother, and, it seems, most of the village, with a rod of iron. She also played the organ. On the plus side, she is remembered as one of the kindest people who ever lived and her chief principle was 'the good of Adlestrop'. She died, aged ninety, in 1947.

Another daughter, Rose Evelyn (1856–1907), was equally lively but in a different way. In 1877, the year before Edward Thomas was born, she was just twenty years old and had spent a year casting a sharp, if somewhat judgemental eye over Adlestrop. She scribbled, in pencil, on half-sheets of paper, her views on 'Its cottages and their Inmates', making no fair copies. These notes remained buried for nearly fifty years until, in 1935, her missionary brother, Lionel, published them privately. Rose did not spare the truth or mince words; she introduces a colourful cast of characters.

The Cholmondeley's coachman lived at the School House with a wife and five children and we are told:

The wife wears her hair in curls, is clean, Low Church, and bad-tempered. The children are tiresome, and have been taken away from our School, as 'Everybody seemed set against them.' Nellie, the youngest, had a piece of a finger pinched off in the School door. The mother, of course, went off into hysterics. She apologized to me for not showing me the piece, but 'Father had taken it in an envelope to show to Captain A.' The finger is now quite right again.

Old Widow Webb has a blind daughter, Bessie,

who is, I'm afraid, no friend of ours. To begin with she has become a rigid dissenter. She has a disagreeable voice and whines about nobody in the world suffering so much as she does.

E.H. lives with his married daughter, her husband and little boy.

E.H. suffers from occasional carbuncles on his neck, but I have nothing particularly else to say about them, so I will pass on to their next-door neighbours, the Reeves's. Reeves is a stout little man, lately returned from Bath, where he went for treatment for his rheumatism. It didn't do him much good, but of course he takes rank on having ridden so far!

I like the sound of Mr Anderson, the carpenter of whom Rose says

we are all fond of him. He is very diffident of his powers, and, if we ask him to do even some small job like mending a window-blind, he will answer softly and leisurely,
    'Yes, we think we can do it.'
Also, in putting up decorations in the Church or, whenever any measuring comes in, he is fond of saying, 'We will mark it with a cedar pencil.'

The Webbs, sadly, 'are to be ranked a slovenly family' but the Haynes' family are

the most meritorious in Adlestrop. . . . Mrs Haynes, or 'Good Maria' as we call her, is our mother's right hand. . . . When anything particular is going on, a School Feast, a Christmas party, or company in the house, she always comes in to help. She can make up carpets, put her thimble on to cover chairs or mend blinds, and is also an admirable sick nurse. Her family is the best brought up in the Village. The children all begin by going out to service at the Rectory, and the younger ones have our old clothes.

This section points strongly to class difference between the House, the Rectory and the village. Marion Haynes, the eldest girl, works her way up from nurse-maid to under house-maid and

> is a gentle-tempered girl and a very good one to attend to the boys when they are home for the holidays. She makes them button-holes on Sundays and bears their scoldings when she hasn't sent their things to the wash or mended them properly.

Poor Marion! There was plenty of washing at the Rectory and most of the village females seem to have handled it at some time . . .

> To Mrs Newman must be accorded the palm of being the best washerwoman in the Village. . . .

but poor Mrs Reeves, wife of an Adlestrop House gardener

> did wash for us for a time but so badly that we gave her up.

Rose thinks that Mrs Willoughby though treated badly must be very trying to live with. She is

> a worn-out little woman, full of ailments and a model of resignation and respectability under the affliction of a drunken husband . . . He looks at you with little owl's eyes and clamps his lips together when he speaks. He says that everybody is always ordering him about, and that he gets treated no better than a lodger . . . for if he comes home late at night, he finds the door locked against him and Mrs Willoughby will not come down to let him in.

She doesn't tell us if he is related to old, widowed George Willoughby, the 'Poet of the Village'. Edward Thomas might have been interested to hear that

> He had a large mourning card made for his wife, bearing a verse on it of his own composition, which he says was revealed to him by night.

Rose turns her shrewd attention on the Howes family:

> The Father is the Clerk, and no one would doubt his being so who sees him in his full black clothes and white choker on a Sunday. He is a worthy man, but wedded to his old ways of doing things, which you cannot bring him to change. In the winter, for instance, he will not put candles in the pulpit at the beginning of the service but, before the sermon, will strike a match behind his clerk's desk and walk solemnly up in front of my Father with two lighted ends of candles, which he places in the sconces. One Sunday, when my Father was pleased with

our singing of a special anthem, which we sometimes attempted, he asked us after the service to sing it again. The old Clerk's account of the matter, when he went home, was

'They sang that piece of theirs so badly today that Mr C had them all back and made them sing it all over again.'

Mrs Howes is one of our numerous washing-women, and perhaps it is the washing that has given her a wheezy chest; she has pushing forward teeth (lately she has lost one) and in talking to us is very respectful and fond of putting in our names.

John Gillett's informative survey of the village in the nineteenth century shows that, as well as the various trades mentioned by Rose, the cottages included a schoolmaster, a carter and butcher, a shoemaker/smith, a postman, a bricklayer, a butler, a maltster, a weaver, and a mason. Both men and women took on extra church duties such as tending the grounds, cleaning, organ upkeep and tuning, and bell-tolling; and a certain Lily Phillips undertook the mending of cassocks, hassocks and surplices from 1909 to 1931 . . . and probably longer.

William Howes, Parish Clerk.

When John Gillett was renovating his own Adlestrop cottage he exposed a large fireplace beam to discover the letters E.T. carved there. A strange coincidence is that his grandfather was called Edward Thomas – no relation. Not surprisingly he named his new home Lob's Cottage, after Thomas's famous long poem 'Lob'. It's a poem rich in the country folk Rose might have recognised, and like her, Edward Thomas had a keen eye and ear for a likely character. Many are to be found in his prose and poetry.

> Women he liked did shovel-bearded Bob,
> Old Farmer Hayward of the Heath, but he
> Loved horses. He himself was like a cob,
> And leather-coloured. Also he loved a tree.

begins one poem; another tells of a Huxter 'with a hump like an ape on his back'.

In one essay is an old countrywoman:

> a tall woman and stooped at the doorway thatch; now she cannot rise to it . . .
> bent like an oak branch on which children swing . . . her flesh seems to have
> assumed an animal sweetness, for her bees will cluster on the brown hands.

In another a country landlord:

> bullied by a contemptuous wife; he was ridiculed by all his regular customers
> . . . he had humour, for he could laugh at himself, tho' he lacked the common
> gift of being able to laugh at others, and had no repartee. . . .

Were either Rose Cholmondeley or Edward Thomas to visit Adlestrop today
looking for a promising subject they would find a vital personality in Dorothy Price.
Looking at the numerous newspapers and magazines in which she features,
journalists and reporters obviously agree.

Mrs Dorothy Price (née Newman, see page 73), known to close family and
friends as Dodie, is at the hub of village life, and is now the only one of the seventy
or so residents to have actually been born in Adlestrop:

> That is a little sad, although all the people are very nice, always friendly,
> always ready to help if you're ill or in trouble. . . .

Dorothy Price. (Photograph by Colin Brent)

Like her mother before her Dorothy was village postmistress – for forty-seven years until her retirement in 1998. There's nothing like a post office for news and local gossip. Edward Thomas and his circle of inveterate letter-writers and post-catchers would have appreciated the part this small, attractive woman has played in Adlestrop where the railway was an important factor in her life:

> My father, Albert Lewis Newman, was a plate-layer from 1912 until he joined the army in 1916. . . .

And Dorothy knew instinctively what I would ask next.

> Everyone wants to know that! Could he have been around Adlestrop Station when that train stopped? . . .

And could he? . . .

> Well, he could, yes, but . . . well, we don't know more than just that.

Dorothy's godfather, Harry Mills, was a signalman, and through her growing-up years she knew all the railway staff. Gathering wild flowers . . . waving at trains . . . these were favourite pastimes. Later on Cyril Price, her husband, worked for the railway too. Their eldest son, Ralph, remembers the day Miss Hill told her class of

Adlestrop Post Office.

eleven-year-olds at Chipping Campden Grammar School in 1958: 'Today you're going to hear a poem that has a connection for you – about Adlestrop.' Ralph asked if he could take the orange-covered anthology home and his 'Look . . . here's a poem about Adlestrop' was the first Dorothy had heard of Edward Thomas.

> And then another day, round that time, Cyril was on the platform when a lady leaned out of the train and asked if he knew the poem. . . . Well, I don't exactly know what Cyril told her, but anyway she said she'd send some copies. And she did. They arrived at the post-office. . . . When I met Myfanwy Thomas . . . you know, the poet's daughter . . . she said 'That must've been Eleanor Farjeon.'

This story sounded suspiciously apocryphal until Dorothy was shown some examples of Eleanor Farjeon's favourite blurred purple carbon copies and recognised them immediately as 'Just like the poems she sent!' Where Eleanor was going in the late fifties I have not discovered. Her memoir, *The Last Four Years*, came out in 1958. Was she, perhaps, revisiting Ryton and Dymock, the haunts of that 1914 summer, as Robert Frost had done in 1957? I don't expect we will ever know.

What I do know, from Dorothy Price, is that since the sixties visitors have come from far and wide to the post office to ask about the poem and where the station is – or was. She directs them to the nameboard in the bus-shelter:

The Parish Meeting put it there in 1966. The bus-shelter was built round it, later, to protect it. School buses stop there and a few others. It was the late Colonel Reeves who had the plaque engraved with the poem and fixed on that railway seat . . . the Reeves family have gone now. . . . Cyril re-painted the board and seat twice. . . . Five years ago boys from the Gloucestershire Probation Service painted it. Ralph got the correct paint, GWR cream and chocolate, from Gloucestershire & Warwickshire Railway – God's Wonderful Railway! – over at Toddington, near Winchcombe. They were reluctant to let him have it at first. . . . Someone rang up one day . . . from Somerset . . . to ask me how to pronounce the name. I told them, like ADDLESTROP . . . well, it did have two D's once. They were really pleased. They'd just found their dream cottage down there and wanted to name it after the poem. . . . Ralph said once 'I don't know why you don't run an Information Bureau, Mother, instead of a Post Office.'

Perhaps, in her retirement, she will. Curious visitors are likely to seek Dorothy Price out for a long time to come. When Cyril retired he devoted two years to making a large detailed scale model of Adlestrop Station. It's about 8 × 4 feet – a skilled and loving piece of workmanship, complete with the station buildings, the bridge, platforms and flower-beds, the railway track and the River Evenlode. And the steam trains. A flashback to the past.

Cyril died in 1990 and Dorothy does look back:

It was busy once, the station, really busy. I can remember milk trains going up to London and in the last war, the Troop trains . . . a lot of people used the station in those days. I love my memories. One day – it must have been in the eighties – Cyril called me, and Ralph, to watch 'The Black Prince' going past . . . steam hissing, like in the old days. It was July. Ralph picked a bunch of meadowsweet and gave it to me and said 'Here you are, Mother; here's a little bit of Adlestrop.'

To Edward Thomas

DIANA ELLIS

Because you remembered,
I, too, will remember
Adlestrop. No train runs
now, but platform sign, large-
lettered, marks the place
where buses sometimes stop.
The air is still and warm,
and willow-herb and grass
smell still as sweet as then,
though five and seventy years
have flowed past with the stream.
Perhaps, if random death
had turned its back on you
in Arras trenches grim,
you would have come again
and loved this tranquil place,
where blackbird still sings sweet,
and casts its spell anew.

1992

Adlestrop Park

ANNE HARVEY

Robert Hartman, best known as a writer for children, wrote his autobiography, *The Remainder Biscuit*, in 1964 when he was sixty-seven. Chapter 1, Beginners Please, opens with:

A thrush is singing outside my window. It is a remarkable thrush, for it has sung throughout the daylight hours of three consecutive days without, so far as I am aware, knocking off for even so much as a passing lunch-time snail. . . .

an opening reminiscent of the lines concluding Edward Thomas's poem 'The Word':

> . . . This name suddenly is cried out to me
> From somewhere in the bushes by a bird
> Over and over again, a pure thrush word.

Earlier in the same poem is the phrase

> – the name, only the name I hear. . . .

with its echo of 'Adlestrop', so it seemed natural in Hartman's chapter on Eton to discover:

> It was while I was at Eton that my parents changed houses; they moved from Hangmoor to Adlestrop Park in the heart of the Cotswolds. I do not think that there exists anywhere in England a more delightful, medium-sized to largish country house than Adlestrop. The house is Jacobean, which classification is almost a synonym for beautiful; it is built of honey-coloured Cotswold stone and looks, from gently rising ground, across a diminutive park, which contains immense elm trees, a cricket ground which is probably the most dangerous in England and a lake fringed, at the far end, with beech trees, which are reflected in the water to form, in autumn a double display of russet and gold. In the distance, silhouetted on the skyline, is the church tower of Stow-on-the-Wold. If this is not the most beautiful view in the world, it is certainly the one that I love most. . . .
>
> The chief feature of the Adlestrop estate was Adlestrop Hill, an expanse of some 400 acres, which had never, so far as was known, been cultivated. A wilderness of centuries-old May trees and rank grass, with paths wandering here and there, a disused quarry, a long stretch of close-cropped turf on which was a pavilion where we sometimes had shooting luncheons, and on the crest of the hill an avenue of beech trees and a small circular Roman camp; such was Adlestrop Hill. For a boy with a gun and a dog there could have been no happier hunting ground.
>
> Alas, Adlestrop Hill is no more; the hill is still there right enough, and so is the Roman camp, but its trees have been pulled up and its character ploughed away. Having survived the First World War, during which gypsies and poachers cleared every single rabbit and pheasant off the place, it succumbed to the demands of the Second World War. I sometimes visit it for old times' sake; as memories come flooding back, I find a lump rising in my throat. And when I look at the house itself the lump grows bigger still, for half the house has been pulled down, and what is left is now a school.

Adlestrop Park was a school for about forty years, and an article in the Spring 1999 Edward Thomas Fellowship newsletter by Bryn Purdy threw more light on this.

Interested in opening a school for disturbed children, Purdy wanted to contact a colleague who had done exactly that but he had lost surname, phone number and school name. One day, in a second-hand bookshop, opening a musty twentieth-century poetry anthology Purdy came upon the poem 'Adlestrop'.

> Adlestrop. . . . Yes, now I remember . . . Adlestrop. Only the name was enough to open a friendship. Now, what was the name of the school? Adlestrop Hall? Adlestrop Park? And where the devil is Adlestrop? Sounds like one of the lost villages of Mercia. But dear old topographically-minded Edward Thomas had provided the clue within the text of the few lines of the poem. The clackety-clack of the train from London to Hereford had surceased, and in the magic silence of that hot June day in 1914 the poet heard '. . . all the birds of Oxfordshire and Gloucestershire'. So that's where Adlestrop is, is it? . . .

Bryn Purdy thus renewed his friendship with Bill Lightbowm who was Principal of Adlestrop Park School from 1967 to 1989. A former pupil, Alena Routh, returning to visit Adlestrop as an adult, remembered being a lonely child and how 'Mr Lighty' showed her 'love and kindness and taught me so much more . . .

> I would sit for many an hour
> On the bench beside the name,
> Adlestrop, the village
> Where rose cottages lined the lane. . . .

Bryn Purdy was well aware of Edward Thomas's poem, as are the present owners of the house, but Robert Hartman made no reference to it. Strangely, though, at the end of the Second World War, the American Army gone from Adlestrop Park, Hartman worked as Press Conducting Officer for GHQ's Public Relations Department, established in the Annexe of the Hotel du Commerce, Arras. And his autobiography ends with this sentence:

> I shall be happy sitting in the garden listening to thrushes singing about whatever it is that thrushes sing about. Nous verrons.

Adlestrop

RALPH MANN

Every year, on the third Sunday in June, the three roads leading into Adlestrop are congested with unwonted traffic. The village, one of the smallest and most remote in Gloucestershire, puts itself on display with a great charity event: Adlestrop Gardens Open. About twenty gardens take part; teas are available in the village hall; home-made jams and cakes are on sale, and of course there is a plant stall. Much hard work goes into the preparation for this event, which is also a small triumph of planning, co-ordination and communal enterprise.

With just over seventy inhabitants, Adlestrop could easily be overlooked. No main road passes through the village; there is no shop or public house and the post office is under threat; the village school and the railway station have long since closed down. And yet the visitors still come. They see the signs, and schoolday memories come flooding back: 'Yes. I remember Adlestrop – the name.'

Adlestrop has never been an important centre. It lies in the upper Evenlode valley, just near enough to the market towns of Stow-on-the-Wold, Moreton-in-Marsh and Chipping Norton to be eclipsed by them. For local government purposes it shares a parish council with Daylesford. And within the diocese of Gloucester, Adlestrop Church was a chapel-of-ease to Broadwell until pastoral reorganisation linked it with Oddington. Imprecise wording of an Order in Council in 1977 unintentionally allowed Adlestrop to claim at last to be an ecclesiastical parish in its own right, with its own elected Parochial Church Council, a decision which brought a new vitality to the Church.

Edward Thomas, of course, never actually saw Adlestrop – only the bare station platform and the haycocks of Lower Farm. Had he alighted and strolled up the footpath past the ornamental lake – a mecca for Sunday morning anglers – and the cricket pitch of which the Adlestrop Cricket Club is justly proud, he would have arrived at the Church of St Mary Magdalene. A series of restorations in the eighteenth and nineteenth centuries has left little of the medieval church for contemplation – the chancel arch, the fourteenth-century west tower, perhaps, the font and some of the lower courses of stonework. Unusually, access is still through the west door, stepping over the half mill-stone which is the last evidence of Adlestrop water-mill, to enter the church below the tower. The bells last rang in 1989, but the bell-frame has shifted and there is no provision for the bells to be lowered for repair. The pews offer generous accommodation – it is hard to believe that there could ever have been a time when the church was regularly filled. The north transept seated the Rector's household, and the south transept provided for the Lord of the Manor, but neither has been used for many a long year. Today,

St Mary Magdalene, Adlestrop.

Sunday services alternate with Evenlode, and the Rector once again lives at Broadwell.

From the sixteenth century, the village has been owned almost entirely by the Leigh family, but the great house which Jane Austen knew is no longer occupied by them, although a Leigh still lives at Fern Farm. After a turbulent period as a private school, Adlestrop Park now belongs to a London businessman who has taken great trouble to restore it to its eighteenth-century splendour. The Rectory, where Jane Austen stayed with her mother's cousin, the Revd Thomas Leigh, is also now in private hands, and is called – confusingly – Adlestrop House. It was here that the Rectors of Broadwell lived from 1672 to 1936, creating the illusion that they were actually Rectors of Adlestrop.

In 1914 most of the inhabitants of the village would have been employed, either directly or indirectly, by the Leigh family, apart from those who worked on the Great Western Railway. Girls would have gone into service on leaving school, and boys went to work on the five farms in the parish. The cottages, though picturesque, were primitive, without running water or proper sanitation.

During the last half century, the village has been transformed just as radically as it was when the farms were created by the Inclosure Act of 1781. Almost all the old village families have moved away, leaving Dorothy Price as the last remaining native-born villager. In their place, incomers have renovated and restored, exposing

the oak beams and the splendid Cotswold hearths, and installing damp courses, central heating and double-glazing. Any gaps in the village (and what other hamlet would dare to call its only thoroughfare 'Main Street'?) have been lovingly filled by houses such as the craftsman-built Honeybrook Cottage, or the fine neo-Caroline Reality House. And in the process, Adlestrop has discovered a new identity. Community spirit is strong, as evidenced by the well-appointed village hall, by the signposted and carefully maintained network of footpaths (leaflet available), and by the traditional carol singing round the village at Christmas. The church fabric and graveyard are maintained with loving care and concern for environmental issues. Discreet, whimsical topiary – a yew cross at the churchyard gate, and a gigantic snail outside Manor Farm – add distinction. The bus-shelter preserves the old station signboard – Adlestrop, just the name – a genuine GWR platform seat, and of course Edward Thomas's poem. And, on the third Sunday in June, there is *Adlestrop Gardens Open*.

A Stroll Around Adlestrop

GORDON OTTEWELL

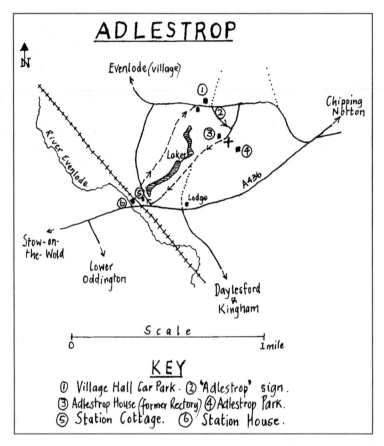

Gordon Ottewell

Distance: 1½ miles

Route: Indicated by dashes and arrows on map

Terrain: Virtually level, along quiet roads and field paths, which may be muddy after rain

Start: Adlestrop village hall car park (OS Landranger Sheet 163 (GR 242272))

Route: Leave the car park and turn left to reach the 'Adlestrop' station nameboard, with Edward Thomas's poem on the platform seat.

Take the right fork. The road climbs gently to reach a junction by the post office. Turn right here to reach the church. Adlestrop House, formerly the rectory, stands opposite.

Go down the lane alongside the churchyard. Pass through a kissing-gate and walk to the left along the perimeter of a cricket field.

The old railway station lies behind the seventeenth-century Station Cottage, which stands on its own in woodland, opposite a fishing lake. Delly and Chris Blane, owners since 1996, are still researching its history and 'like to think that it was the birds in our garden that inspired one of the verses in Edward Thomas's poem.'

Follow the drive towards a lodge on the A436. On reaching a clump of oak trees on the right, leave the drive to follow a sunken path to the left of the trees. This crosses the park to reach a road over two stiles.

Turn right here. The drive to Station Cottage on the left is a former approach road to the station. Station House stands on the opposite side of the track.

Continue past the lake to reach a stile on the right. The footpath from this stile leads back to the village round field edges. On reaching a road, turn right back to the village hall and the start.

John O'Connor

Adlestrop Now

ALAN BROWNJOHN

The name, as I drove west that day,
Flashed from a hedgerow. Since the sign showed
Only two miles, having time enough
I took the little winding road

Along to the village. First I passed
A wood, and then a field where straw
Burnt black, and near a notice-board
Which said 'Neighbourhood Watch', I saw

Two well-trained citizens staring hard
At me, and at my number-plate.
Alarms clung to cottage walls, and locks
Guarded each wild-rose porch and gate,

And after a brief stay, I thought
I'd go. I had no wish to stir
Rumour in all those covered nests
Of Oxfordshire and Gloucestershire.

1987

My Adlestrop!

MIKE SHARPE

*Almost any man may like the spider spin from
his own inwards his own airy citadel.*

This is Keats' view of creativity expressed in a letter to his friend John Reynolds on 19 February 1818. In the same letter, he draws a distinction between the merely mechanical 'knowledge' of memory and the creative 'knowledge' that memory can release.

For the past two years, I've been working with patients at several psychiatric day-hospitals to help them release something of this creative knowledge. I've been a kind of visiting writer running 'creative writing' sessions for patients (or clients) on a weekly basis as part of their programme of occupation therapy.

Recently, this work has been under the auspices of GOFAL CELF or ARTS CARE, a project in West Wales designed to provide a planned programme of artistic activities for mentally ill people in day-care centres and hospitals.

It's always rather surprising that people so readily sign up for an activity with the label 'Creative Writing'. It's an off-putting title but there's no really adequate alternative. No title quite fits this particular pen-in-hand activity and, in any case, nobody else seems as sensitive as I am about the name. For many who attend, it's simply an activity that's not woodwork or art or kitchen-management.

And yet it's so much more. There's an enhancing magic about it which shows itself unbidden and so unexpectedly.

For an hour or so people sit at tables absorbed in something that they last did, probably with great reluctance, in English lessons at school. And here they are, in adulthood, finding a new impetus to language, a willingness to struggle on paper with words, in a process that might have been left permanently impaired by the inhibitive nature of the formal education some of them have experienced.

A session is like a pool of quiet. There's nothing to disturb us, no urgency, no pressing demands or responsibilities. The world is outside somewhere and excluded. Memory and imagination are free to range unpressured and unchallenged. How rarely do any of us find ourselves in such a circumstance!

We focus for a while on a poem, a painting, a photograph, some music.

. . . I remember on one occasion introducing Thomas Hood's bitter-sweet poem 'I remember, I remember' I'd hardly had time to hand round some copies when a rather shy member of the group suddenly began to recite it in that incantatory way school-learnt poems are often spoken. After many years, the words had surfaced again (to some spontaneous applause). I mention it because it illustrates everybody's instinctive relish for the moods of language. In my experience, it is manifestly possible to blend that pleasure in words with a rediscovery of the power that words can exercise.

I took in, one day, Edward Thomas's 'Adlestrop' to illustrate how a moment can be unexpectedly and unintentionally momentous. One member of the group took to the idea with enthusiasm. As a child, he frequently travelled by rail from Leicester to Birmingham (I think to his boarding school) and one station-sign captured for him all the associations that journey had. He would greet my arrival each week with the cry:

> 'Water Orton! Water Orton!
> My Adlestrop!'

I don't think he realised he had an Adlestrop before he discovered the possibility in Edward Thomas's poem.

POETRY REVIEW, 1995

Remembering Adlestrop

HERBERT LOMAS

I too remember Adlestrop—
that compatible weekend in the car
when all the birds of Gloucestershire
seemed intoxicated by tar

and dawdled on the road. I slowed
to let them loop away. 'Adlestrop
must be somewhere here,' I said.
Then, towards dusk, a sudden stop:

a signpost: 'Adlestrop!' I cried,
not really having looked, and turned.
No railway; just the station sign,
yellow, conserved, and I somehow yearned

and grieved as a blackbird sang.
Had I an inkling even then that now
I'd hear it with a wringing pain,
knowing your love had stopped, not how?

Linda Holmes

Farewell to Adlestrop

FROM A CORRESPONDENT

Casting my eye down Dr Beeching's list of condemned stations in England I paused at the fifth name: Adlestrop. True, its high rank on the list was only an alphabetical placing; but to me it seemed important. Yes, I remember Adlestrop. . . .

To some readers, nurtured on more turgid or knotty verse, Edward Thomas's poem may even be unknown. In any case it is worth quoting now that the Beeching plan has added an extra note of sadness to its music:

Yes. I remember Adlestrop—
The name, because one afternoon
Of heat the express train drew up
   there
Unwontedly. it was late June.
The steam hissed. Someone cleared
   his throat.
No one left and no one came
On the bare platform. What I saw
Was Adlestrop—only the name
And willows, willow-herb, and grass
And meadowsweet, and haycocks dry,
No whit less still the lonely fair
Than the high cloudlets in the sky.
And for that minute a blackbird sang
Close by, and round him, mistier,
Father and farther, all the birds
Of Oxfordshire and Gloucestershire.

Thomas was killed in the First World War but it must have been a year or two after the second one had ended that I first saw Adlestrop station. Holidaying in my stationary caravan on a Buckinghamshire hilltop, I had grown sated with the Chiltern backcloth, had pumped up my bicycle tyres, told my wife not to expect me for a couple of nights and headed for the Cotswolds, almost unvisited since boyhood. Approaching Stow-on-the-Wold, I lazily pushed my cycle over a bridge, glanced down at the railway station below and read on its board a name which until then I had thought of only as the title and subject of a poem.

RETURN VISIT

What particularly delighted me was that quite apart from such associations, Adlestrop station was well worth looking at. Its flowerbeds, shrubs and trees were obviously tended with affecionate care. I felt immediately that the staff knew of the poem and were determined that their station should be worthy of it.

My map told me that the stream flowing beside the station was the river Evenlode. As I lingered at the spot I determined to come again with my wife, whose enthusiasm for Edward Thomas first sparked off my own interest.

An opportunity to do so arose the following winter when we were out with relatives on a motoring expedition from north London (in those days one could go motoring for pleasure in England) and my brother-in-law, recalling with gratitude that I used to do the same for him in my own car-owning days, handed the wheel to me and told me to drive where I liked. I think everyone except my wife thought it a little odd when I finally pulled up outside a railway station and insisted that they must get out and look at it properly, merely because someone had written a poem about it, but they duly admired the scene and we warmed ourselves up by walking round the village, led by my niece and sister at a run.

It was a long time afterwards, in 1959, that I travelled on a Sunday excursion to visit my younger sister at Stourbridge, in Worcestershire. I had not studied the train's route and supposed that we should go as usual via Birmingham. Actually we had long passed Oxford when I awoke from a doze to find the train at a standstill. A strange feeling impelled me to a corridor window. Looking back I saw, just beyond my coach, a station platform. . . .

No one left and no one came
On the bare platform. What I saw
Was Adlestrop—only the name.

It was too early in the year for meadow-sweet and willow-herb and too late in the morning for all the birds of Oxfordshire and Gloucestershire; but there it was, unchanging and peaceful beside the Evenlode.

FINDING A TRAIN

How disappointed I was when, having greeted my sister with the news that my express had drawn up 'unwontedly' at Adlestrop, I had to explain to her about the poem, which she did not know.

By now I was living in Kent. That summer circumstances prevented me from going away on holiday. But, determined on at least a one-day change of scene, I decided to find a train that really stopped at Adlestrop, not 'unwontedly' but on purpose. My A.B.C. guide was not much help:

ADLESTROP (Glos.)–87$^{1/2}$ miles. From Paddington. Second class 14s. 8d., first class, 22s. Local trains from Kingham, 5min. extra journey, or Oxford, 55min. extra journey.

My telephone call to Paddington took a long time. I had to be insistent and some research was necessary at the other end. It appeared that nearly all Adlestrop's few trains called there in the early morning or evening; but at last I established that if I travelled on a Thursday it was possible to arrive there at noon.

And that was how I came to prove to myself that it was possible, in what we must now call the pre-Beeching era, for a resident of Kent to spend a leisurely day in Cotswold country with no strain of driving or fuss of coach booking. All my travelling time was spent comfortably reading in a corner seat.

I enjoyed wandering around Adlestrop, where a county library van was delivering books – how pleasant, I thought, to retire to one of those cottages and collect my reading matter from a van. I enjoyed roaming through Daylesford and Oddington and Stow-on-the-Wold. But most of all I enjoyed arriving at that beautifully tended station. When I handed in my ticket I did not ask the stationmaster whether he knew Edward Thomas's poem. Perhaps I was afraid of breaking a spell.

Now the economy axe is breaking the spell for hundreds of Adlestrops throughout Britain as we move into the era of the coach crawl and (if Miss Rachel Carson's warning is not heeded) the silent spring.

THE TIMES, 5 APRIL 1963

The Search for the Other Nameboard

ANNE HARVEY

Adlestrop was finally closed on 3 January 1966, and The Times *followed the story . . .*

Adlestrop Remembers

British Railways recently muffed a chance of keeping alive the memory of Edward Thomas and his poem on the little Gloucestershire village of Adlestrop. Though the Oxford to Worcester line remains open, Adlestrop station was scheduled for demolition. The North Cotswold RDC asked the railway to leave the nameboards so as to remind passengers of a poet who was killed in the battle of Arras in 1917 and of an afternoon in June when he looked out of a railway carriage window to see why his train had stopped at a wayside station. British Railways remained sternly unmoved. The RDC's request was refused and the two nameboards were delivered at the Council's offices – transportation fee 10s. Suggestions as to what should be done with them have included a proposal that one should be placed in the garden of Lincoln College, Thomas's Oxford College.

THE TIMES, 7 MAY 1966

They Remember Adlestrop

There has been a happy ending to the controversy as to what should be done with the nameboards from Adlestrop's dismantled railway station, inseparably connected with Edward Thomas's poem. After consultation between the North Cotswold RDC and the poet's widow, one of the nameboards has been erected at the entrance to Adlestrop village whose parish council has found an old GWR platform bench to accompany it. First choice as a destination for the second nameboard was the Railway Museum at Swindon; but Swindon was not interested, so the board has found an honoured home in the Lettering Museum of the College of Technology at Oxford.

THE TIMES, 15 AUGUST 1966

Sadly that is no longer true because the Oxford College of Technology no longer exists. Few appeared to have heard of it, or of John Henry Brooke's vision for further education for the ordinary folk of Oxford and district. Then it transpired that Oxford Brookes University had inherited the courses and retired Art Lecturer Harry Crook explained the numerous changes that had taken place over the years

since 1954. I discovered that, in 1966, a lecturer in Book and Magazine Publishing and Production, Gerald Wilkinson, had been the driving force behind the sign collection. My hopes were raised until I read:

> When in recent years, fine art had become once again a specialised subject all the wall space was required for assessment and so no signs were taken to be displayed in the new building. Those that were left were mainly enamel hoardings such as 'Pratt's Motor Oil'. One cast iron railway platform notice was sold to Didcot Railway Museum, the rest were given away. I think I can safely say that if ADLESTROP was ever in the collection it didn't remain for long.

Mr Crook went on to explain that he'd worked under five different Heads of School . . . and a new member of staff would 'rip out practically all fittings and fixtures and put his or her own stamp on the room to effectively wipe out all that had gone before.' He did add 'All is not totally lost' and his colleague, Dennis Hall, recalled Gerald Wilkinson's sign collection quite well:

> The smaller shop and street signs I put up in the building but there was a large sign for ADLESTROP station which was too large to go inside and we hoped to fix it to the outside of the building but the Director objected to this and it remained I think in the summer of 1970 or 1971 leaning against an alcove of the building where we hoped to install it. In the summer the caretakers removed it when everyone was away. I imagine they burnt it. Not much more to the sad tale. Gerald Wilkinson was killed in a car accident a few years ago so we can't find out how he came by the sign.

Harry Crook wrote again:

I was thinking – even if the brown and gold up-platform notice board presently at the bus stop at Adlestrop is contemporary with Thomas it may not be the actual one he saw. It all depends on his position in the carriage and where the train came to a halt to cool down. I imagine it was on its way to Oxford otherwise it wouldn't have overheated but that is probably already known as fact. . . . I must confess that I am more interested in the sign than the poet. I think that unless it is the actual noticeboard that prompted the poem, well you might as well paint one yourself. Best wishes and good hunting. . . .

Wood engraving by Ray Hedger.

This, That and the Other

CAROLE SATYAMURTI

Yes. I remember Adlestrop—
The name . . .
            Edward Thomas

We're so programmed to the binary
(this, or that; that, not this) we slip
into exhausted possibilities like shoes:
left, right. Butt them neatly.

Think of all those unnamed states:
between fear and lust, say, between
hope and disappointment, art
and its imitations, bud and flower.

Even this *and* that brings on headaches;
neither this *nor* that is territory
we pass through yawning,
confused, waiting to arrive.

If naming is poets' work, even without
a board, announcing, would he have
given us that exemplary window of words,
slant on all nowheres in particular?

Or, irritably registering delay,
would he have dozed,
leaving us deaf to all the birds
of Oxfordshire and Gloucestershire?

Charles Tunnicliffe

And for that moment a blackbird sang
Close by . . .

Only the Name

(*based on* Adlestrop)

DANIEL JONES

Yes I remember Adlestrop
The name because one afternoon
A man stood alone on a platform
Unwontedly it was late June.

His appearance I do not remember
He walked to the edge as the in-train came
A few feet away from the waiting crowd
Was Adlestrop only the name.

And everyone saw what was coming, too late
Or at least had some notion
Like a football crowd they looked away
His jump was like slow motion.

And willows, willow herb and grass
And meadow sweet and haycocks dry
Were no less fair and lowly
Nor did anybody cry.

The shaken driver trembled out
The station master took off his hat
Wiping his brow 'God this is a mess'
As if looking at a trampled cat.

And for that minute a blackbird sang
Close by and mistier
His jump that day was all the talk
Of Oxfordshire and Gloucestershire.

The gossip about the man that died
Itself died down and all was the same
All they knew of him were the words on the ticket
'Mr Adlestrop' only the name.

*Daniel Jones was a prizewinner in Shell's 1991 Young Poet of the Year
Competition. Thirteen at the time, he said: '"Adlestrop" was one of the first
really good poems I read and although I still don't know much about Edward
Thomas it is the only poem I could recite from memory.' Strangely, he did not
know Edward Thomas's essay 'Death by Misadventure' (1911), published in*
Cloud Castle *in 1922.*

Death by Misadventure

EDWARD THOMAS

As the train slowed down between the long grey platforms all the men in the
carriage dropped their newspapers to their knees and raised their eyes,
without any appearance of thought or emotion, in short with a railway-carriage
expression, to scan the name of the station, the small groups by the bookstall, the
two or three intending passengers just coming through the doorway of the
booking-office. On steeply rising ground above the station flocks of white linen
flapped wildly and brightly in the back gardens of rows of new cottages. Above

these, white clouds went nobly through the sky like ships ages ago on some long quest of love or of war.

When the train was still, there was not one shout. No one called out the name of the town or the place for which we were bound. No one cried 'Chocolate,' 'Paper' or 'Violets' though the vendors of these things were at hand a moment ago.

A stout man in black coat and black gaiters opened the door of our carriage and got in puffing, yet saying as he closed the door:

'Man killed. Carelessness. Nobody's fault except his own. Teach platelayers a lesson. Smoker and drinker, I'll be bound.'

People began to hurry past our windows towards the engine. Those in the carriage who sat nearest the windows put their newspaper on the seats and in turn put out their heads to look. 'You can't see anything,' said one.

The train backed slowly a few yards. 'He was under the engine,' said the observer. Some of us were dimly pleased to have had an experience which not everyone has every day; the stout man was disturbed by the delay; others were uncomfortable during this movement, as knowing that they were in part the cause of the accident and that their weight was now helping to crush out the blood and life of a man; one wanted to jump out, but while no one was willing to leave the carriage, all were bent on taking their turn at the window.

A policeman walked smartly by, and one of the seated passengers remarked that 'on the Continent' they arrest the engine-driver as a matter of course. Two porters followed with a stretcher.

'Now they are picking him up, but I can't see for the crowd,' said the one who now had his head out. 'Here he comes. . . . No. He must be dead. . . . There is some more.' The train backed yet a little again. 'They have got all of him.'

In the little gardens the housewives and daughters were already watching. Old and young, buxom and slender, fresh and worn, in their white aprons and print dresses, leaned over the low fences, one stood upon the fence and stared. The scent of death had not taken a minute to reach those women whose sons and husbands and fathers and lovers include some – it is not known which of them – who are destined to die bloodily and unexpectedly. There was not a sound except the hissing of the steam, until the guilty train began to grunt forward again and take us past a little group of uniformed men with ashen faces surrounding the brown humpy cloth which covered the remains of the chosen one.

Adlestrop

(*after Edward Thomas*)

SIMON RAE

*This week the Government published a White Paper announcing the
privatisation of British Rail under a franchise system.*

Yes, I remember Adlestrop,
Boy, do I remember Adlestrop!
That's the bare platform where my train
Came to an unwonted stop.

Passengers hissed; some spat.
But no trains went and no trains came.
The guard, who had a brochure, said
It seemed to him a crying shame

But no one yet had stumped up cash
For the franchise. He shook his head.
Fact of the matter was, the line,
The line ahead, our line, was dead.

Perhaps we'd like to seize upon
This opportunity to see
Some shares – no whit less valuable
Than those let's say of B-Sky-B?

No? He shrugged and we sat looking out
All afternoon, as hours dragged by,
At willows, willow-herb and grass,
And meadow-sweet, left high and dry.

And suddenly it seemed to me
All the transport infrastructure
Ground to a halt in that backwater
In Oxfordshire, or Gloucestershire.

WEEKEND GUARDIAN, *18 JULY 1992*

A New Train of Thought As We All Go Off the Rails

PETER TORY

Long interludes in pastureland are increasingly the lot of those who travel by British Rail. The train slows and halts. There is silence. Nothing is explained. The cows continue to graze. A dog barks. A farmer's wife at a gate over the meadow calls her husband for his tea. The world goes by. Shares rise and fall. And so on.

Such an unscheduled halt occurred at Pevensey and Westham, East Sussex, the other day. Driver Steve Toughie was well aware that a signal-box fire up ahead would delay his twenty passengers for at least an hour. So what did he do?

Before we consider Mr Toughie's unusual show of initiative, it might be worth recalling that celebrated poem about a similar delay at a little rural halt in Oxfordshire.

Instead of Pevensey and Westham, read Adlestrop. It's much the same. And, at the time of the poet's experience, it was a hot day too.

Yes. I remember Adlestrop—

Those of us who have taken a railway train – and that is most of us – will feel that they, too, have been to Adlestrop. But the tranquil and enchanting pleasure expressed by the poet is, surely, a thing of journeys past. If you stop in the fields nowadays, you don't listen to the ruddy larks, you rage and fume like a madman.

So what did driver Steve Toughie do to pacify his passengers? Let them listen to the songbirds? Not a bit of it. He took them all to the pub, that's what he did.

After clearing his plan with his headquarters by telephone, he led the passengers to the Pevensey Castle Hotel and, while abstaining himself, spent £35 on drinks. The passengers were well pleased and Mr Toughie's bosses were delighted. This really is an astonishing business. May it not be that the incessant yearly heatwave weather is leading to the Latinisation of the British character. You need look no further, for proof, than British railway travel.

Today commuters tug angrily at the knots of their ties, shrug furiously at each other, gesture at the heavens and strike up animated conversations about the complete disintegration of society.

And on top of it all we now have the splendid sight of a driver abandoning his train, and marching the passengers off to the local inn. This is what you would expect on the 19.43 out of Milano.

Oh Adlestrop, Adlestrop, where be your serene magic now?
Actually – and I saw it the other day – the white on
brown GWR station board is still in place. There is no station.
No railwayline. Just the name Adlestrop.

THE DAILY EXPRESS, 15 AUGUST 1995

Adlestrop Retrieved

MARTIN NEWELL

Great Western Railways have made certain carriages on their day-time services
mobile-phone-free zones. They have also barred personal stereos from end
carriages.

Bombastic brash and over-prone
To shouting on his mobile 'phone
He's cancelling his three-o-clock
Or booking tickets for Bangkok
So fellow travellers have no choice
But hear his self-important voice:
'I've godda window, Tuesday. Noon.
'Yup. Abso-lootly. Speaktcha soon.'
No sooner has he closed the thing,
His brief-case then begins to ring.
And down it comes from off the rack.
'I'm breaking up. I'll call you back.'
As fellow travellers wish he'd stow
His mobile phone where phones don't go.
And so the pompous prat proceeds
From Paddington to Temple Meads.

But something just as wearing is
The tiska-tiska-tiska fizz
Of Walkman-wearing younger chap
In baggy trews and baseball cap
Whose headphone volume range can spill
From Very Loud to Louder Still
It's bad enough from town to town
But torture if the train breaks down.

Had Edward Thomas known this lout
His poem would not have come out
And all we'd know of Adlestrop
Was that the train had had to stop
For if that bird had deigned to sing
This would have been the only thing
The poet heard close by and brisker:
'Tiska-tiska-tiska-tiska . . .'

THE INDEPENDENT, 10 APRIL 1996

Adlestrop Revisited

A.D. MELVILLE

No. They've forgotten Adlestrop—
No platform now to show the name;
No sign of any station left,
Only the shining rails the same.

And the old station-master's house,
And photos in the porch to show
The little station and the staff
In uniforms of long ago.

It was a day in early June,
Quiet, and not a soul in sight,
A soft and sleepy afternoon.
Just the cow parsley foaming white

And buttercups and dandelions;
And in the willows by the rails
Thrushes and tits and warblers sang—
And later, maybe, nightingales.

To Adlestrop

JIM TURNER

Never again a train will stop
Unwontedly at Adlestrop,
Nor hissing steam awake and stir
The poet's fine-spun gossamer.
Salvaged and sheltered, the station sign
Hangs on his own immortal line.
But willow-herb and meadowsweet
Still mingle where the meadows meet,
And ecumenical at will
Oxford and Gloucester birds sing still.

Half-hidden down the narrow road,
Most lovely named, lies Evenlode
Broadwell-the-beautiful hard by
Under the cloud-flecked Cotswold sky
And every road that climbs the wold
Goes back to Stow, where winds blow cold.
Four counties spread their riches still
Around the sky-borne, tree-topped hill.
Islanded high, old landmarks ride,
Bright in the evening's ebbing tide.

Edward Thomas in Heaven

P.J. KAVANAGH

Edward, with thinning hair and hooded eyes
Walking in England, haversack sagging, emptied of lies,
Snuffing and rubbing Old Man in the palm of your hand
You smelled an avenue, dark, nameless, without end.

In France, supposing the shell that missed
You and sucked your breath out as it passed
Released your soul according to the doctrine
You disbelieved and were brought up in,
From slaughtered fields to Christian purgatory?
(Assuming your working life, the sad history
You sweated through, and marvellous middens of rural stuff
You piled together were not purgatory enough?)
Are you now a changed person, gay and certain?
Your eyes unhooded, bland windows without a curtain?
Then it would not be heaven. It would be mere loss
To be welcomed in by an assured Edward Thomas.
There must be doubt in heaven, to accommodate him
And others we listen for daily, who were human,
Snuffing and puzzling, which is why we listen.
How shall we recognise the ones we love
If next we see them fitting round God's finger like a glove?
While close-by round him, mistier,
Farther and farther, all the birds
Of Oxfordshire and Gloucestershire
And angels of Breconshire and Hereford
Sing for them, and unimaginable Edward?

1974

ACKNOWLEDGEMENTS

Acknowledgements and thanks are due to the following authors, publishers and agents for permission to use copyright material.

John Loveday for 'The Imaginative Franchise' from *Particular Sunlights* (Headland, 1986); Simon Hoggart; Gervase Farjeon for extracts from Eleanor Farjeon's *Edward Thomas: The Last Four Years* (OUP, 1958/Sutton Publishing, 1997) and *The Green Roads* (The Bodley Head, 1965); R. George Thomas for extracts from *Letters to Gordon Bottomley* (OUP, 1968) and *Selected Letters of Edward Thomas* (OUP, 1995); Gordon Ottewell for an extract from *Warde Fowler's Countryside* (Severn House, 1985) and for 'A Stroll Around Adlestrop' (1999); William Cooke for an extract from *Edward Thomas: A Critical Biography* (Faber, 1970) and for his poem 'Adlestrop Revisited'; John Bayley for a passage from 'The Self in the Poem' from *The Art of Edward Thomas* edited by Jonathan Barker (Poetry Wales, 1987); Myfanwy Thomas for part of her introduction to *Poems, 1917* (Imperial War Museum, 1997); Susan Hill for a quotation from *The Spirit of the Cotswolds* (Michael Joseph, 1988); David Higham Associates for 'Do you Remember Adlestrop?' by Norman Nicholson from *Sea to the West* (Faber, 1981); Monica Hoyer for 'Actually Adlestrop?' 'What he Heard' and 'Single to Adlestrop' from *Single to Adlestrop* (1993); Michael Horovitz for 'Not Adlestrop' from *Wordsounds & Sightlines: New & Selected Poems* (Sinclair-Stevenson, 1994); Julian Ennis for 'Names'; Leslie Norris for an extract from *A Land Without a Name* (Poetry Wales, Vol. 13, No. 4, 1978); the estate of the late John Adlard for an extract from ARCHIV, (London, 1980); Douglas Verrall for 'Applestrop'; the estate of the late Harry Coombes for an extract from *Edward Thomas: A Critical Study* (Chatto & Windus, 1956/1973); B.S. Beezer for 'Adlestrop' from *Adlestrop Remembered* (1992); Sean Street for 'The Poem and the Place' (1999); Brian Patten for 'Lockerbie' from *Armada* (Harper Collins, 1996); Francis Berry for 'Vadstena' from *Ghosts of Greenland* (Routledge, 1966); Peter Porter for 'Good Vibes' from *Living in a Calm Country* (OUP, 1975); Roland Gant's estate for a section of his introduction to *The Prose of Edward Thomas* (Falcon Press, 1948); Roger Frith for scenes from his play 'Adlestrop'; Dannie Abse for 'Not Adlestrop' from *A Small Desperation* (Hutchinson, 1968); C.R. Potts for a passage from *An Historical Survey of Great Western Railway Stations*, Vol. 4 (1985); Chloe Edwards for 'The Train'; Desmond Elliott, Administrator of the Estate of Sir John Betjeman, for 'Back to the Railway Carriage' from *Coming Home* (Vintage, 1998); Chris Turner for the article 'The Bare Platform'; Diana Ellis for 'To Edward Thomas' from *Adlestrop Remembered* (1992); Andre Deutsch Ltd for an extract from Robert Hartman's *The Remainder Biscuit* (1964); Hardiman Scott for 'Adlestrop' from *When the Words are Gone* (Chatto, 1972); John Gillett; Dorothy Price; Ralph Mann for his article 'Adlestrop' (1999); Alan Brownjohn for 'Adlestrop Now' from *In the Cruel Arcade* (Sinclair Stevenson, 1994); Mike Sharpe for an extract from *My Adlestrop!* (Poetry Review, 84, No. 1, 1995); Herbert Lomas for 'Remembering Adlestrop'; *The Times* for 'Farewell to Adlestrop' (1963), 'Adlestrop Remembers' (1966) and 'They Remember Adlestrop' (1966); Carole Satyamurti for 'This, That and the Other' (1999); Daniel Jones for 'Only the Name'; Simon Rae for 'Adlestrop' (*Weekend Guardian*, July 1992); Peter Tory and the *Daily Express* for 'A New Train of Thought' (August 1995); Martin Newell for 'Poetic Licence' (*Independent*, April 1996) A.D.

Melville for 'Adlestrop Revisited' from *Adlestrop Remembered* (1992); P.J. Kavanagh for 'Edward Thomas in Heaven' from *Edward Thomas in Heaven* (Chatto/The Hogarth Press, 1974).

Thanks also to the following for invaluable quotations, letters and comments:

Christopher Somerville; Jane Asher; Fiona Cumberpatch; Peggy Poole; Johnny Coppin; Antonia Fraser; Margaret Drabble; Richard Ingrams; Christopher Reid; Boyd Tonkin; Andrew Motion; John Carey; Griff Rhys Jones; Geoffrey Palmer; Stephanie Cole; Jill Hyem; Roger Frith; Dame Judi Dench; Bill Peto of the Great Western Society Ltd; Oliver Lovell, Promotions Officer, Cotswold Line Promotion Group; Anne Pope, Tom Colverson, Harry Crook and Denis Hall (for information on the Adlestrop name-board); Grenville Simons; Bryn Purdy and Alena Routh.

Particular acknowledgement is due to the following for permission to use archive material:

The Manuscript Department of the British Library for the manuscript copy of Edward Thomas's poem 'Adlestrop';
The Berg Collection of English and American Literature, the New York Public Library. Astor, Lenox and Tilden Foundations for quotations from Edward Thomas's Field Notebook dated June 1914;
Lincoln College Library, Oxford, for access to the research archive of the late Ramon Willey

Sally Brown and Christopher Fletcher at the British Library, Stephen Crook and Wayne Furman at the Berg Collection, and Fiona Piddock and Alexandra Wynn at Lincoln College, Oxford, have all been exceptionally helpful and my thanks go to them all and also to:

Gaye King of the Jane Austen Society for her most welcome advice; Viv Beeby and Christine Hall from the BBC's *Poetry Please* programme; Bee and Walter Wyeth and Chris Hill from The Pitshanger Bookshop; and to the Edward Thomas Fellowship, the Friends of the Dymock Poets, the Folio Society, the Poetry Society, Ealing Reference Library, and the Public Records Office.

Adlestrop Revisited owes a great deal to my many friends, old and new, whose faith and support have helped to make my literary investigations a pleasure:

Myfanwy Thoma, Gervase Farjeon, Gordon Ottewell, William Cooke, R. George Thomas, Dorothy Price, John Gillett, Chris Turner, and Ralph Mann have been especially patient – as have my editors at Sutton Publishing, Jaqueline Mitchell and Clare Bishop.

The book could not have happened without any of them, or the following:

John Barnes, Delly Blane, Andrew Boreham, Colin Brent, Mick Campion, David Eddershaw, Richard Emeny, Richard Furstenheim, Frances Guthrie, Linda Hart, Simon Hoggart, Jinnie Holt, Patrick Ingram, Alan Martin, Kim Plested, Sean Street, Edward Cawston Thomas, Steve Turner, James Harvey Woolliams and Douglas Verrall.

PICTURE CREDITS

Discovering paintings, wood engravings, and drawings of 'Adlestrop' has been a great joy to me and I thank all the artists for the interest they have shown and for adding a different dimension to the book. I must especially thank Linda Holmes, John O'Connor, Birtley Aris and Neville Morris for their generosity.

I have made every effort to contact copyright holders and apologise for any omission. Sources are as follows (page references to this anthology are given):

'Adlestrop' by James Bostock from *These Things Also Are Spring's* © The Folio Society Ltd, 1988. London, 1988: ix; © Myfanwy Thomas: x, xi, 26, 61, 103; from the Farjeon Estate: 5, 7, 8, 16; © James Harvey Woolliams: 13; © Ramon Willey's archive, Lincoln College, Oxford: 14; © Estate of Gwen Raverat, 1999. All rights reserved DACS; cover illustration for A.G. Street's *Farmer's Glory* (Faber, 1932): 15; © Michael Gibson: 17; © Bernard Brett and the Bodley Head; illustration from *The Green Roads* (1965): 23, 67, 81, 107, 112; © Linda Holmes: 28, 100; © John O'Connor; wood engraving for Richard Ingrams' *England* (1989): 30, 97; © Estate of Robin Guthrie: 32; © Neville Morris: 34; © Paul Howard & Walker Books, London, 1998: 36; © Birtley Aris, from a collection of Edward Thomas inspired drawings for a travelling exhibition, 1980s: 41, 53; © Oxford University Press, 1958. Reproduced by permission: 48; © Adrian Vaughan: 60; © David Hanks: Cotswold Images: 65, 86, 88, 94, 95; © A.F.H. Austen: 77; © Colin Brent: 87; © Gordon Ottewell: 96; © Delly Blane: 97; © Ray Hedger; wood engraving from Johnny Coppin's *Forest and Vale and High Blue Hills* (1993): 104; Blackbird Singing from *The Seasons and the Gardener* by H.E. Bates (Cambridge, 1940). © The Estate of C.F. Tunnicliffe: 105.

FURTHER READING

Although many of the titles mentioned in the text are out of print and only available through catalogues and second-hand bookshops the following are available:

Under Storm's Wing – Helen Thomas's two books, *As It Was* and *World Without End* in one volume (Carcanet Press, 1997)
Edward Thomas: The Last Four Years by Eleanor Farjeon – re-issue edited, with new material, and introduced by Anne Harvey (Sutton Publishing Ltd, 1997)
The Dymock Poets by Sean Street (Seren Books, 1994)
Collected Poems of Edward Thomas (OUP (1981) and Faber (1979) editions)
Edward Thomas: A Portrait by R. George Thomas (OUP, 1985)

The Edward Thomas Fellowship and the Friends of the Dymock Poets can be contacted at:

Edward Thomas Fellowship
Hon. Secretary Richard Emeny
Butler's Cottage
Halswell House
Goathurst
Bridgwater
N. Petherton
TA5 2DH

Friends of the Dymock Poets
Secretary Linda Hart
7 Winston Close
Ledbury
Herefordshire
HR8 2XQ